TROUBLEMAKERS
AND
SUPERPOWERS

KEELY GRAND

Illustrated by
RAGON DICKARD

little bigfoot
an imprint of sasquatch books
seattle, wa

For Ben and Ely, and my nieces and nephews, Anna, Eliza, Emma, Jack, Maggie, and James—I love you all. And to all the kids out there who interact with and experience the world differently, who've been faced with troublemakers, and who are finding their superpowers! —K. G.

For you, hurt and hurting, confused and yearning. You are not alone. —R. D.

ACKNOWLEDGMENTS
Special thanks to my husband, family, and friends for lifting me up and supporting me on my journey. Thank you to Michelle McCann for believing in me and this project. Thank you to Dr. Jill Waldman, Dr. Malkah Notman, MD, and Marisela Van Sickle, LCSW, and Basil Wright for sharing your incredible knowledge and expertise to ensure accuracy, sensitivity, and empowerment within these pages. And a heartfelt thank-you to all of the people in the world who have shared their stories in order to help others. —K. G.

Manufactured in China by C&C Offset Printing Co. Ltd. Shenzhen, Guangdong Province, in June 2023

LITTLE BIGFOOT with colophon is a registered trademark of Penguin Random House LLC

27 26 25 24 23   9 8 7 6 5 4 3 2 1

Editors: Michelle McCann, Christy Cox
Production editor: Peggy Gannon
Designer: Tony Ong

Library of Congress Cataloging-in-Publication Data
Names: Grand, Keely, author. | Dickard, Ragon, illustrator.
Title: Troublemakers and superpowers : stories of 30 people who turned childhood struggles into strengths / Keely Grand ; illustrated by Ragon Dickard.
Description: Seattle, WA : Sasquatch Books, [2023] | Includes index.
Identifiers: LCCN 2022043685 | ISBN 9781632173003 (paperback)
Subjects: LCSH: Determination (Personality trait) in children--Juvenile literature. | Children with social disabilities--Juvenile literature. | Abused children--Juvenile literature. | Success--Juvenile literature.
Classification: LCC BF698.35.D48 G736 2023 | DDC 155.4/19--dc23/eng/20230217
LC record available at https://lccn.loc.gov/2022043685

ISBN: 978-1-63217-300-3

Sasquatch Books
1325 Fourth Avenue, Suite 1025
Seattle, WA 98101

SasquatchBooks.com

TABLE OF CONTENTS

Foreword **5**   Introduction **6**

Understanding the Keywords in this Book **7**

Dr. Maggie
 Aderin-Pocock 10

Shane Victorino 14

Ed Sheeran 18

Emma Stone 22

Thurgood Marshall 26

Howie Mandel 30

Frida Kahlo 34

Michael Phelps 38

John Green 42

Nora Lum
 a.k.a. Awkwafina 46

John F. Kennedy 50

Greta Thunberg 54

Bobby Herrera 58

Trevor Noah 62

Hamish Brewer 66

Clay Marzo 70

Joe Grand 74

Jonathan Van Ness
 a.k.a. JVN 78

Seane Corn 82

Tariq Trotter
 a.k.a. Black Thought 86

Daymond John 90

Joy Harjo 94

Simone Biles 98

Ayanna Pressley 102

Dr. Temple Grandin 106

David Goggins 110

Josh Fernandez 114

Dav Pilkey 118

Alecia Moore
 a.k.a. P!nk 122

Afterword **126**   Resources **126**   Index **127**

FOREWORD

NOTE TO KIDS:

Hi! You obviously don't know me, and I don't know you, but what I do know is that you're probably curious about the lives of the people in this book. You may be interested in learning the stories behind all they've accomplished or finding out what life was like for them when they were younger. Or you may be a kid who is struggling with troublemakers—such as OCD, dyslexia, or anxiety—that the subjects in this book struggle with. Or you may be a family member, classmate, or friend of someone who you know is experiencing these struggles. Sometimes it can be hard to relate to or understand kids you may have observed interrupting, blurting out answers, or getting in trouble a lot. Or maybe you've noticed kids being especially shy or frustrated in a way that doesn't make sense to you. No matter what brought you here, I'm glad you are here. The world needs more people seeking to understand themselves and also one another. I hope that when you finish reading these stories, you feel inspired. Because no matter where you are in your life's story, every human has a worthy place in this world.

Like many of the kids I work with, learning and discovering what it's like to live with mental health disorders, learning disorders, or any sort of struggle can be quite challenging. It's common to feel misunderstood, and maybe even inadequate, in explaining how you feel and how you need help. But what I've seen time and time again for many years is that most kids get to a crossroads: they either let the "troublemakers" win or they fight back. Kids that fight back learn to focus on what they are able to do rather than what they're not able to do. They accept help from their support team, and they learn to advocate (without shame or embarrassment) for their needs. Sometimes it may feel like a two-step forward, one step back kind of fight, but hang in there.

There are subjects in some of these biographies that touch on heavy experiences such as abuse, divorce, addiction, racism, classism, and more. It's common for various life experiences to exacerbate mental health disorders and even learning disorders, and for many, it's not possible to talk about one without the other. If you find yourself overwhelmed or impacted by one of the stories, please reach out to a trusted adult and process your feelings together.

As you read these biographies, I encourage you to keep thinking about your next chapter: What new and exciting thing will you do next in your life story? If you have your own troublemakers, how are you going to push back against them? Know that you have so many people rooting for you. The truth is that everybody has needs. And we all deserve to feel seen, understood, and loved for who we are.

In strength and support,
MARISELA VAN SICKLE, LCSW

INTRODUCTION

I'd like to first take a moment to acknowledge the local Indigenous tribes of the land I grew up running around on—the Narragansett, Nipmuc, Niantic, Wampanoag, and Manissean tribes—as well as the local Indigenous tribes of the land my family and I currently run, work, and live on—the Cowlitz, Clackamas, and Confederated Tribes of Grand Ronde, and the Confederated Tribes of Siletz Indians.

The idea for this book brewed from my oldest son's struggles in school. I was constantly being told about the trouble he was creating, and although I acknowledged his disruptive behavior, I also knew that there had to be a reason why he was struggling so much. Why was he the "class clown"? Why was he frustrated? Why was he having meltdowns and crippling fear at home? What was going on with my funny, sensitive, happy kid?

When my son was nine years old, my questions were answered. After comprehensive testing, he was diagnosed with obsessive-compulsive disorder (OCD), and later, his therapist included attention deficit hyperactivity disorder (ADHD). I finally knew the why, and through the years, my husband and I would learn how to properly support him. Through therapy, skills he's learned, and a new school that sees his strengths and supports his growth, he is able to be an active listener and learner in his classes.

The process of discovery we went through as a family led me to wonder about what other people went through in their childhoods, which then led me to write this book. It became my quest to help kids with troublemakers, like OCD, in their life, and to shine a light on the superpowers within

us all. Also, another goal was to encourage people to develop more understanding for those of us who may seem different from what society deems "normal," and I hope that this book helps those who seek understanding.

When this book was near its final stages, my youngest—who is nonbinary, sensitive, and insightful—was diagnosed with dyslexia, dysgraphia, and dyscalculia. All of it made learning extremely challenging for them and also explained why they were in tears every day before and after school. The research I had done for this book gave me the knowledge and strength to help them succeed despite the trouble they were facing.

I know firsthand as a mom with kids who have differences, and as someone who has also tangoed with my own anxiety and ADHD my whole life, how challenging the journey can be. But I also know that it's going to be OK. We all have challenges that can help us to see our gifts, and I hope that this book helps kids and adults understand their differences, the differences in others, and leaves them inspired by the fact that our differences make the world a better place.

In this book, you will find stories about people who faced some sort of trouble or silent struggle in their life, had a turning point, and became successful in their ambitions. Some people are well known, and some are not, but they all have incredible stories that I hope will help any reader feel comfort, kinship, and confidence to become whomever they want to be and to do whatever they wish to do.

—KEELY GRAND

UNDERSTANDING THE KEYWORDS IN THIS BOOK

There are some words in this book that you may be curious about. I've defined those words below, but because every person and their experiences are different, these things may feel different to you. If any of these keywords apply to you and are interfering with your daily life, please consider talking with a trusted adult and seeking professional help and support.

ABUSE: When someone is harmed verbally, emotionally, sexually, and/or physically through violence, force, or by coercion. It's not normal or OK. When someone's personal boundaries are broken, they can suffer in many ways. Common components of abuse are an abuser's use of coercion, threats, intimidation, and bullying. Often, the abuser will isolate the person they are abusing, act possessive of that person, minimize the feelings of that person, deny they are doing anything wrong, and blame the person they are hurting. There are times when abusers can act nice or warm, but it is usually followed by periods of engaging in abusive behavior. This can be very confusing. It is important to let a trusted adult know if someone is making you feel uncomfortable.

ADDICTION: A disorder that creates a compulsive dependence or need for a thing, activity, or a substance like drugs or alcohol, despite the negative effects it has on a person. Addiction is treatable, and people can recover with the right support.

ANXIETY: A common and normal reaction to stress. Anxiety can cause someone to feel an emotional response, like fear, worry, dread, and discomfort, and a physical response, like an increase in heart rate, sweating, stomachaches, shakiness, crankiness, and hyperawareness.

ANXIETY DISORDER: When a person's brain has persistent feelings of worry that they can't control that affects their daily life. Inside their body and mind, a person could have a constant feeling of worry or panic, restlessness or feeling "on edge," tiredness, nervousness, or brain fogginess. People can also experience trouble with sleeping, have stomach problems, may avoid certain activities, and/or can have a hard time staying focused because of their worrying. One out of every five kids has a mental health disorder, and the most common are anxiety disorders.

ATTENTION DEFICIT HYPERACTIVITY DISORDER (ADHD): A condition that can cause someone to have difficulty concentrating and poor working memory. It can also include hyperactivity and impulsivity, such as excessive talking and doing things without thinking first, and having excess energy that makes it hard to keep your body still or calm even when you want to. It's common for someone with ADHD to have an intense interest and pour their energy into that interest, sometimes creating the inability to focus or give attention to other things.

AUTISM OR AUTISM SPECTRUM DISORDER (ASD): The characteristics of autism and its range of severity vary greatly. Most people living with autism spectrum disorder generally struggle socially. Commonly, kids who are on the autism spectrum can struggle with reading and understanding the behaviors, feelings, and expressions of others. They may be inflexible in their thoughts and behaviors and often will perform repetitive behaviors, called "stimming," by flapping their hands, rocking, spinning, repeating words, or humming to reduce their anxiety. A person with autism may also avoid eye contact, have restricted interests, and have uncomfortable sensations and reactions to sounds, smells, tastes, textures, lights, and colors.

DEPRESSION: A common and normal feeling that anyone can experience. It's normal for people to feel sad and depressed because of loss, failures, and disappointments.

DEPRESSION AS A DISORDER: When depression regularly affects daily living, it is considered a mental health disorder, and it deeply affects someone's mood. People with this mental health disorder usually struggle with a constant feeling of sadness, hopelessness, and a loss of interest in all or most of their daily activities. Feelings of worthlessness or guilt are also common. In children, significant irritability or crankiness sometimes occurs more often than feelings of sadness.

DYSLEXIA: Difficulty with reading and figuring out how letters work and sound. Specifically, dyslexia is a struggle with understanding or visualizing letters and how they go together to make words. This can make spelling and reading a challenge. Some kids find that their head gets tired, and sometimes they get headaches when they are practicing writing and reading skills.

DYSGRAPHIA: Difficulty with gathering one's thoughts and putting them down onto paper. There can be a struggle with expressing thoughts in writing as well as with punctuation and grammar. It is common to have both dyslexia and dysgraphia.

DYSCALCULIA: Difficulty with learning and understanding math and numbers. The effects can be different for each person struggling with dyscalculia.

EDUCATIONAL TRAUMA: When learning and teaching practices at school negatively affect a student. The experience could lead a student to slow down their learning or stop it altogether. This could be caused by teachers not supporting you, other students making fun of you, or embarrassment when not understanding an assignment, lesson, or subject.

NEURODIVERSITY/NEURODIVERGENT/ NEURODIVERSE: A term used to explain that there are different ways that the human brain can work. The differences in how brains work can make life challenging, but they can also help people recognize their strengths because they interpret and respond to the world in unique ways. Some examples of neurodiversity are dyslexia, ADHD, and ASD.

OBSESSIVE-COMPULSIVE DISORDER (OCD): OCD is made up of two components: obsessions, the intrusive thoughts, or "bully thoughts," that cause anxiety (an intrusive and constant "what if?"); and compulsions, behaviors, or mental rituals to bring the anxiety down (an answer/solution to the question). When OCD is unmanaged, it can be time-consuming, bossy, and a huge disrupter to life. The more someone listens to the intrusive thoughts, the bigger OCD gets. When OCD's bossiness is ignored, it gets smaller and smaller.

When Maggie Aderin-Pocock was six years old, growing up in London, England, she saw a book about an astronaut floating in space with the view of Earth, the only known planet to possess life, off in the distance. It was a magical love-at-first-sight moment for her.

She was captivated by the TV shows *Cosmos* and *The Clangers*, which introduced her to the universe, home to about a hundred billion galaxies. To this day, she is dazzled by the expansive sea of stars and by the notion that there may be life other than humans out there.

Maggie is a space scientist with advanced science degrees. There have been people who have second-guessed her because of the color of her skin and because she is a woman. Luckily, she never let people's opinions and thoughts get in the way of her life's purpose–exploring the universe through the lens of a giant telescope and sharing the excitement of science with people of all ages.

Although she was brilliant when she was young, she didn't always feel smart. In fact, she felt dumb. Reading and writing were excruciatingly difficult for her. She had an exceptional imagination, but she grew frustrated with herself because she couldn't translate her thoughts to paper. Maggie was diagnosed with dyslexia, a learning disorder that involves challenges with reading, when she was eight years old. Her struggles with reading and writing were frustrating for her, so she often just sat in the back of the classroom feeling upset.

Teachers didn't try to help her, and they didn't show interest in her, so she took every opportunity to make kids laugh, acting like the class clown. Even when she expressed her dream of becoming a space scientist, many teachers mocked her. The only person

"MAYBE I'M NOT STUPID. WHAT ELSE CAN I DO?"

who seemed to always believe in and encourage her was her dad.

One day, her education took a magical turn in a science class. Her teacher asked the class a tough science question, and Maggie immediately knew the answer. She shot her hand up to the sky, but no one else's hand was raised. Second-guessing herself, Maggie lowered her hand. But something inside of her told her she was right, so she raised her hand again and got the answer correct!

Science was the key factor in building Maggie's confidence. She finally felt like she was good at something, and it was something she really liked. With her newfound interest and skill, Maggie was inspired to read everything she could about science. And all that effort she put in ended up helping her in her other subjects, too, and, in time, Maggie was excited about school.

Another challenge Maggie faced was her parents' divorce. She was only four years old when she and her siblings were caught between her parents' battles over where the children would live. As a result, they bounced back and forth between homes, and Maggie attended thirteen different schools before the age of eighteen. Despite her struggling family life, she found comfort in science.

Her curiosity for space encouraged her to save up her allowance to buy her very own telescope. It failed her expectations, so she enrolled herself in an adult class for telescope making. She was the youngest in the class by far, but she joined these older stargazers in building a telescope that met her standards!

"I FOUND THE BENEFITS OF DYSLEXIA, SUCH AS GOOD 3D SPATIAL AWARENESS AND A STRONG LOGICAL SENSE, WHICH WERE IDEAL FOR A CAREER AS A SPACE SCIENTIST."

Maggie also struggled with a sense of belonging. Her parents were from Nigeria, but she grew up in England. She never felt like she was a part of either place. Nowhere felt like home. Throughout her life, she was one of the few Black kids in school, and with each advanced degree she earned, there were fewer people who looked like her. It was lonely, which is why, as an adult, she works to change mindsets and inspire kids to study science regardless of race, gender, or learning challenges.

Maggie initially thought that she'd study theoretical physics like Einstein. Dyslexia made that challenging and forced her to approach her education differently. She shifted to a more hands-on approach. She went to college to study physics and furthered her education by getting a PhD in mechanical engineering.

Although she moved through much of life with undiagnosed dyslexia, Maggie sees her differences as gifts. Her gifts afford her 3D spatial awareness and a supreme sense of logic. Combined with her bright personality, she has been able to contribute so much to the world. She hosts a children's TV show and cohosts BBC's *The Sky at Night*, and has written two books, including one for children.

Maggie has contributed to creating land-mine detectors and measuring the rate of climate change using space satellites and has worked with both the European Space Agency and NASA. Her love for building telescopes, like NASA's James Webb Space Telescope, may be a dream come true, but her most treasured work is speaking to kids and impassion their interest in science.

"IN SPACE, RACE DOESN'T MATTER, NATIONALITY DOESN'T MATTER.

IN SPACE, YOU SEE THE WORLD AS A GLOBE AND YOU DON'T SEE THE BOUNDARIES."

A professional baseball player between 2003 and 2013, Shane Victorino is known as the Flyin' Hawaiian. He was an extraordinary outfielder who could be seen diving, jumping, and chasing down any ball without fear.

Before he was in the major leagues, Shane was an energetic and physically gifted kid growing up on Maui in Hawaii. However, he didn't have the ability to be in control of his impulsive mind, which landed him thirty stitches and ten hospital visits all before the age of eight.

He was fidgety and bouncy when he needed to sit still. He couldn't contain his impulse to lash out with his words or control his body even as early as preschool. Since learning was already proving to be a struggle, his mom ultimately decided that he'd be better supported in a special learning center rather than a traditional school setting.

Shane's behavior boggled his mom's mind. Why would a kid take their seat belt off, open a moving car's door, and fall out without being afraid of getting hurt? Even after barreling down the street on his bike and getting hit by a car, Shane was more worried about his bike and possibly getting into trouble than he was about pain, seeing blood, or breaking bones.

His dad saw himself in his son. He remembered how often he got into trouble and couldn't sit still. He understood what Shane was going through and tried to talk to him about it. However, Shane's impulses were too big. His family needed help.

Shane was diagnosed with attention deficit hyperactivity disorder (ADD/ADHD) at five years old. Shane received support through therapy, medication, and patient and understanding people.

"THAT'S HOW OUR CULTURE IS IN HAWAII. OUR CULTURE, WE'RE ACTUALLY WARRIORS. POLYNESIANS ARE WARRIORS BY NATURE. A WARRIOR WILL BATTLE THROUGH ANYTHING AND EVERYTHING."

—SHANE'S BIG BROTHER MIKEY

Patience and understanding aren't easy to ask of anyone when they see a kid throwing a tantrum in the middle of a game. However, Shane's natural talent for sports was undeniable, and every coach wanted him on their team despite his lack of control.

Shane's older brother, Mike, was also good at sports, and regardless of being more than four years older, Shane tried hard to be as good as him. Like most little brothers, Shane looked up to his big brother. Mike recognized the impact he had on his little brother. So he not only supported his talent but also helped him develop a strong work ethic. He made Shane understand that working hard was important to becoming the best he could be.

Shane's inability to think before acting would often cause

benches to clear, resulting in fistfights with opposing teams. Most people only saw the hot, quick-tempered athlete. They thought he was overconfident and had a bad attitude, but it was his ADHD that caused his impulsivity. After games, he'd often go with his mom to her second job cleaning offices. He was thoughtful and sweet, but most people didn't get to see that side of him.

Despite the battle to control his emotions on the field, sports played a huge role in Shane's mental health. Sports gave him an opportunity to be laser-focused on something. With each season came a new sport, helping him to channel his energy and focus into something productive.

The older Shane got, the more control he had over his emotions. One day, his mother expected Shane to explode during a soccer match when he got a yellow card

as a warning and then a red card ejecting him from the game. She closed her eyes, waiting to hear signs of him losing control, but they never came. Instead, he sat on the bench calmly talking to his coach.

High school proved to be a turning point for Shane. Major League Baseball scouts showed interest in him. Maui wasn't known for producing professional athletes, so it was surprising to have scouts around. His mom cautiously began to see that professional baseball could be in her son's future.

In 2003, Shane played in his first professional baseball game with the San Diego Padres. During his career, he also played with the Philadelphia Phillies, the Los Angeles Dodgers, the Los Angeles Angels, and the Boston Red Sox. Even as an adult, he was interrupting his teammates and still feeling agitated by the roller coaster of emotions he was feeling during a game. So he had to find solutions to cope.

Therapy; preparation; music, which helps him relax and focus; and sticking to a routine are big components to Shane managing ADHD. His boundless energy and impulsivity may have been too much for some, but the very things that made him different helped him achieve his dreams in sports. With the right support, Shane was able to figure out how to be his best self and do what he loved. Shane retired from baseball in 2018 and spends his time with his family and creating opportunities for youth through his charity.

As a young boy, English singer-songwriter Ed Sheeran was shy, wore oversize glasses, and had a stutter. He also considered himself to be a bit weird. He was an easy target for bullies and came home from school nearly every day crying because kids made fun of the way he looked and spoke.

Ed tried everything the doctors told him to do to eliminate his stutter, but it persisted. He eventually stopped talking altogether at school because he was sick of being hurt.

Before high school, Ed's school experience was overshadowed by athletes and sports, and he couldn't identify with either. He was left feeling uninspired, lonely, and different from everyone else.

Although he detested school, his home was full of art, music, and love. He and his brother spent their time painting, playing with LEGOs, or practicing instruments. Eventually, Ed taught himself how to play the guitar!

When he was ten years old, Ed got hooked on the bestselling rapper of all-time, Eminem, and his 11x platinum album *The Marshall Mathers LP*. He was hypnotized by Eminem's melodic rap style. With relentless practice, he learned every word of every song on that album, and ended up correcting his stutter in the process! It was a huge feat for him and one less thing to get bullied over.

High school was more interesting and less lonely. There were more kids with varied interests. Ed was able to find people who shared his interests and a place where his quirkiness was accepted rather than rejected.

Although he fit in better, he still had no interest in school. It was a struggle for him to get there, never mind to stay in class or do homework. But he was all in with music. Music had helped him overcome his stutter and had grown to become a huge part of his life.

"I'M PROOF THAT PEOPLE AREN'T BORN WITH TALENT."

Instead of battling Ed's strong pull toward music, his dad encouraged him to participate in it. He took Ed to concerts and to places where he could perform on his own.

One artist who had a monumental impact on Ed was Damien Rice. Not only was Ed a big fan, but Damien was also the first singer-songwriter Ed saw live. He loved the idea of playing on stage with just an acoustic guitar and singing a song he'd written himself. Damien even took time after a show to talk to Ed, which inspired him to try writing his own songs. Ed will tell anyone that he wasn't born with talent, but he had determination. With relentless practice, Ed's skills began to improve. Always striving to beat his own best, he worked hard and pushed himself to become a better musician than he was the day before.

One night, Ed went to see one of his favorite bands, Nizlopi. The opening act was a music artist named Gary Dunne, who performed using a looper pedal. A looper pedal allows a musician to record themselves both instrumentally and vocally and can then play back what was just recorded in a loop. Discovering the looper pedal helped Ed realize that he didn't have to have a band accompany him; he could be a solo musician. With the unwavering support of his parents, the tenacious young musician quit school and hit the road with his guitar at the age of sixteen. He played on the streets, in clubs, and basically anywhere people would listen. He traveled all over, sleeping on different couches every night. He was playing hundreds of gigs a year and recording in between gigs. His songs were gaining him fans on iTunes

"JUST BE YOURSELF 'CAUSE THERE'S NO ONE IN THE WORLD THAT CAN BE A BETTER YOU THAN YOU, AND IF YOU TRY TO BE THE COOL KID FROM CLASS, YOU'LL END UP BEING VERY BORING."

as well as some money, but still, record companies didn't offer him a contract.

He continued to play, caught the interest of Elton John and Atlantic Records, and was even invited to sleep on actor Jamie Foxx's couch and use his recording studio. People dug his music, but no contract came his way.

But Ed persisted in his pursuit to be a successful musician. His turning point came after uploading his album *Collaborations* to the Internet. He woke up the next morning to find his music sitting at #2 on the iTunes charts. Many record labels called that day. Contract offers came streaming in. Some companies offered more money than others, but Ed ultimately chose Atlantic Records.

Ed's success as a musician is off the charts, just like his work ethic. He has set impressive goals for himself, all of which he has accomplished. He was different. He was bullied. And he had one single intense interest—music. He followed his interest to the fullest and became not only one of today's leading musical artists, but he also created his own record label to give new artists a shot at making their dreams come true. Ed knows what it's like to feel, look, and sound different than others, so he publicly shares his childhood differences to encourage others to be proud of their uniqueness and to be themselves!

With big green eyes and a smile that goes for a mile, Emma Stone is a lasting star in Hollywood. She grew up in Scottsdale, Arizona, and was surrounded by love and support from her brother and parents.

From the outside, Emma appeared to be like any kid her age. But inside, she wasn't. Emma lived with a lot of fears and worries, even reaching a point where she couldn't go to friends' houses or she'd need to ask over and over what the plans were for the day, or the next day, or the day after. She had no control over her big fears and worries. When she was seven, her parents decided to find the reason why Emma had such intense fears. It turned out that Emma had an anxiety disorder.

Although her parents didn't tell her she had a disorder, Emma was aware that there was an annoying pest called anxiety that was constantly making her worry. Anxiety can feel noisy and bossy in your mind. It can begin with one pesky worry that turns into a whole mountain of worries. You could feel sweaty, or your heart could beat faster. Maybe your worries feel so big, you freeze. And maybe you feel so much fear that you can't think clearly.

Through therapy, Emma had someone to talk to and learned that she could reduce her anxiety. She drew pictures of her in control of her thoughts and minimizing anxiety's power. Before long, those drawings were real—she was able to gain control and manage her anxiety.

Along with therapy, Emma found an activity that helped with her anxiety. Acting! She put on shows in her house and bossed her little brother around as her creative assistant. At age eleven, Emma joined the Valley Youth Theatre in Phoenix. Though her sensitivity

EMMA WAS AWARE THAT THERE WAS AN ANNOYING PEST CALLED ANXIETY THAT WAS CONSTANTLY MAKING HER WORRY. ANXIETY CAN FEEL NOISY AND BOSSY IN YOUR MIND.

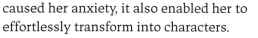

caused her anxiety, it also enabled her to effortlessly transform into characters.

She loved acting so much that it became her sole interest. One day, she used a PowerPoint presentation to convince her parents to allow her to be homeschooled so she could focus on acting. It was no secret that acting meant a lot to Emma, but because it also proved to ease her anxiety, her parents agreed.

Improv was a favorite of Emma's, and she would play any acting role she could get, big or small, because when she was acting, the worries disappeared. Acting forced her to be present in the moment, and when that happened, her mind couldn't wander.

In just a few years with the Valley Youth Theatre, Emma had played a part in twenty different performances, like *Alice in Wonderland*, *A Winnie-the-Pooh Christmas Tail*, and *Princess and the Pea*!

Although talented, Emma was a bit of a handful. Her youth theater teacher, Bobb Cooper, took notice of Emma's natural acting ability and became an important teacher in her life. Emma was very talkative and often stole the show, even when she wasn't on stage! Still, Bobb was one of her greatest teachers and inspirations. She credits her success not only to her family but also to him.

At fourteen, Emma created another persuasive presentation. It involved leaving home and the Valley Youth Theatre. She invited her parents into her room and sat them down with some popcorn. She showed them another PowerPoint presentation titled "Project Hollywood." Her dream was to move to Los Angeles and become a Hollywood actor. Again, it was all she could think about. Not only did her parents see the transformation acting had on Emma and her anxiety, but they also recognized her

"HEY, I WANT YOU TO ALWAYS REMEMBER: IF SOMEONE DOESN'T GET YOU, THAT'S NOT ON YOU, THAT'S ON THEM. IF THEY DON'T GET YOU, THEY'RE NOT YOUR PEOPLE."

—DOUG WALD, EMMA'S MANAGER

passion and talent for it. So her parents agreed to her new plan, and a few months later, she and her mom moved to Hollywood.

In Hollywood, Emma got a manager, Doug Wald, who was very supportive of her, but she struggled to get roles. She went to audition after audition, and nothing worked. She was rejected and found herself working odd jobs, like baking dog treats. Her manager and parents encouraged her to be herself and keep trying.

Eventually, she landed the role that would jump-start her Hollywood career. It began with a teenage comedy,

Superbad, and has continued with *Battle of the Sexes, La La Land, Easy A, Cruella,* and other great projects. She stayed focused and worked hard to reach her goals. Her advice to everyone pursuing their dreams: "Never give up."

Emma still struggles with her anxiety, but she has the tools to help herself, such as therapy and meditation. She believes that if people don't let anxiety suck them in and instead put their energy toward something they're super interested in, then it can be a "superpower."

THURGOOD MARSHALL
LAWYER, SUPREME COURT JUSTICE

"EACH OF YOU AS AN INDIVIDUAL MUST PICK YOUR OWN GOALS. LISTEN TO OTHERS BUT DO NOT BECOME A BLIND FOLLOWER. DO NOT WAIT FOR OTHERS TO MOVE OUT — MOVE OUT YOURSELF — WHERE YOU SEE WRONG OR INEQUALITY TO INJUSTICE SPEAK OUT, BECAUSE THIS IS YOUR COUNTRY, THIS IS YOUR DEMOCRACY — MAKE IT — PROTECT IT — PASS IT ON. YOU ARE READY. GO TO IT."

Thoroughgood Marshall was born in 1908 in Baltimore, Maryland. He was a sweet but disruptive kid who was always up for a debate. He convinced his mom to legally change his name to Thurgood when he was entering elementary school. His argument—"Thoroughgood" was too long for him to write!

Between the ages of two to six, Thurgood and his family lived in Harlem, New York. There he was nicknamed Goody, and his house was nicknamed the Friendly Inn, as Thurgood, who was slight and shy, would bring home Harlem's stray animals, hungry kids, and strangers with him for food and a nice place to sleep. But others saw him as weak. The neighborhood kids would tease him and slap his head, and his aunt would refer to him as a crybaby. So, he grew tougher, ditched his nickname, and demanded that everyone call him Thurgood.

His family moved back to Baltimore, where Thurgood began first grade. In school, he was no longer the timid kid he once was in Harlem. Instead, he was loud and full of energy, consistently disrupting his classes.

From a young age, with eyes wide open, Thurgood witnessed racism and the inequalities inflicted on the Black community. The ongoing battle for equal justice surrounded him throughout his life. Thurgood grew up during the time in US history when segregation—unfairly keeping people of color separate from white people in schools, neighborhoods, transportation, and businesses—was a legally and socially enforced plague in everyday life.

Thurgood's all-Black high school was jam-packed. It didn't have a cafeteria,

gym, or library. It was so small that half the kids went to school in the morning and the other half in the afternoon. Thurgood was fully aware that the all-white schools had money, space, and everything they needed for kids to learn, while Black schools did not.

In high school, his desk overlooked the local police station. Not only did Thurgood get an education watching the station, but it was one of the things that got him in trouble. He couldn't stop himself from interrupting the class to tell everyone what he was seeing! For his disruptions, he was sent to the basement to read the US Constitution. And not only did he have it memorized by the time he graduated, but he also began to understand the law in a different way because of it.

Thurgood was a great debater. He started out debating with his dad, as his dad was very interested in the law and would sit in the back of courtrooms and observe trials. Their debates proved to sharpen Thurgood's growing craft as he was named captain of his high school's debate team every year he participated!

He followed his brother to Lincoln University in Pennsylvania for college. He had a great time with friends, playing card games, and carrying on with his spectacular storytelling. He was the loudest student by far, and his carefree attitude caused most of his schoolmates to consider him the least likely to succeed. Just like in high school, he enjoyed the debate team the most. He even earned a spot on the varsity team as a freshman!

We the People of the United States,

o Article XIVo

ALL PERSONS BORN OR NATURALIZED IN THE UNITED STATES, AND SUBJECT TO THE JURISDICTION THEREOF, ARE CITIZENS OF THE UNITED STATES, AND OF THE STATE WHERE THEY RESIDE. NO STATE SHALL MAKE OR ENFORCE ANY LAW WHICH SHALL ABRIDGE THE PRIVILEGES OR IMMUNITIES OF CITIZENS OF THE UNITED STATES. NOR SHALL ANY STATE DEPRIVE ANY PERSON OF LIFE, LIBERTY, OR PROPERTY, WITHOUT DUE PROCESS OF LAW; NOR DENY TO ANY PERSON WITHIN ITS JURISDICTION THE EQUAL PROTECTION OF THE LAWS.

> "DEMOCRACY JUST CANNOT FLOURISH AMID FEAR. LIBERTY CANNOT BLOOM AMID HATE. JUSTICE CANNOT TAKE ROOT AMID RAGE. AMERICA MUST GET TO WORK."

Within a few years, Thurgood began to take school more seriously. After initial resistance because of their opposing views, he slowly became friends with the prolific writer Langston Hughes, whose world travels had shaped his deep understanding of people, culture, and world issues. Thurgood learned from Langston's writing, lectures, and close relationship with the National Association for the Advancement of Colored People (NAACP)—a civil rights and social justice organization founded in the early 1900s that works to bring equality, justice, and equity to Black Americans.

At the age of twenty, Thurgood fell in love and got married. In 1930, he graduated college with his eyes set on law school. Segregation denied him from being admitted to the school of his choice, so he chose Howard University School of Law. He quickly rose to the top of his class and won the affection and mentorship of the most influential Black lawyer of the time, Charles Hamilton.

Thurgood graduated first in his class, and after establishing his own law firm, he joined the NAACP and eventually became their chief legal counsel.

Thurgood was smart, crafty, and calm in his work to end racial segregation. Most importantly, he was true to the law and earned the title Mr. Civil Rights. In 1954, he overturned "separate but equal" in the critical Brown v. Board of Education case. His response when asked what he considered equal was: "Equal means getting the same thing, at the same time, and at the same place." This historic case was the foundation of building the Civil Rights Movement. Two years later, Rosa Parks wouldn't give up her seat on an Alabama city bus, which was followed by Dr. Martin Luther King Jr.'s movement for equality.

In 1967, President Lyndon B. Johnson appointed Thurgood Marshall to the highest court of our nation, and he became the first African American to join the Supreme Court of the United States.

HOWIE MANDEL
COMEDIAN + TV PERSONALITY

"I HAVE THE BEST FAMILY – EVERYONE SHOWS ME NOTHING BUT LOVE, SUPPORT, AND STRENGTH. EVEN WITH ALL THAT, IT CAN BE HARD – SOMETIMES TERRIFYING AND DARK – TO MANAGE THE SYMPTOMS OF MY DISORDERS."

Howie Mandel is a comedian and cohost of the TV show *America's Got Talent*. He loves to be entertained and loves to entertain.

From the moment his baby brother was born, to compete for his parents' attention, Howie would do nearly anything for the spotlight. It didn't matter if the attention he got was positive or negative, he just wanted all eyes on him.

School in Toronto, Canada, was both lonely and fun for Howie. It was fun for him because school was his stage. He was constantly trying to make everyone laugh, but no one did. All he got out of them were eye rolls.

Howie was impulsive to the point where kids didn't want to be friends with him because he was constantly getting in trouble and was often more annoying than he was funny. He had little to no control over his impulsive behavior.

However, his parents were very supportive of him. When he'd run into their bedroom at night to try out a funny voice, they'd stop whatever they were doing, listen, and laugh. Years later, a voice he tried out with his parents actually became the voice Howie used for the character Bobby in the cartoon *Bobby's World*!

Comedy albums, variety shows, and cartoons were always playing in his house, but one show in particular made a huge impression on him, *Candid Camera*. This was a hilarious show where cameras were hidden to catch the reactions of unsuspecting people in odd

"WHEN I WAS GROWING UP, MY SYMPTOMS DIDN'T HAVE A NAME, AND YOU DIDN'T GO TO A DOCTOR TO FIND OUT. SO, IN MY CASE, THEY WERE CALLED HOWIE MANDEL."

and uncomfortable situations. The people were part of a joke, and they didn't know it. Howie loved this show so much that he'd go around town and do things to people as if he were the star of *Candid Camera*, except he wasn't—he was the only one in on the joke!

When Howie wasn't pulling pranks, he was worried about germs, specifically germs in the air, like coughs and sneezes, and germs coming in contact with his hands. He spent a good portion of his childhood with his shoelaces untied because he could absolutely not touch dirty shoelaces.

In his adulthood, Howie would learn that his irrational fear of germs was caused by obsessive-compulsive disorder (OCD). In Howie's case, OCD was very disruptive to his daily living and occasionally was debilitating.

The older Howie got, the bolder he was with his pranks and the more extreme his fears became. Sometimes his fear of touching or breathing in germs would temporarily control his life. If a door was shut and he didn't have a glove with him, he'd find creative ways to open the door that didn't involve using his hands.

OCD may have caused him to live with a lot of fear, but he has always been fearless in his comedic pursuits. Howie's impulsive behavior and stunts were wildly funny in his mind, but other kids didn't think so until his high school years. The kids who accepted him in those years are still his best friends today.

His pranks got him kicked out of three high schools because his teachers weren't aware of his challenges. At one school, he called a bunch of contractors to come to the school and give quotes to expand the library. At another, he left a lone candy bar floating in the swimming pool to look like poop. During his third try at another high school, he managed to get expelled for impersonating one of the school's board members.

Howie's personality, although trouble at school, was anything but trouble at work. His impulsiveness and sense of humor helped him to become a hugely successful carpet salesman.

He'd answer his business phone in different voices to make it seem like more than one person worked with him. When he'd go to a customer's house, he always tried to make them as uncomfortable as he could, like taking off his shirt and drawing a floor plan on his stomach! He got to perform his own comedy every day, and nobody questioned him!

Howie really found his groove when he started doing stand-up comedy. Worries melted away the minute he took the stage, and he finally found his connection to people in professional comedy.

His work in stand-up comedy led to work in TV shows and movies. Though his mind is often racing more than he is, and he lives in a state of discomfort more than not, he feels unburdened when he's in the spotlight, and that's been a good thing for him. He navigated more than forty years of his life before he was diagnosed with ADHD, OCD, and anxiety. His conditions can interfere with his life, but he has a loving and supportive family and manages his symptoms by going to therapy and taking care of his health. He's outspoken about his mental health, and he hopes his story will help others through their own challenges.

"I THINK THE SOLUTION TO MAKING THIS WORLD BETTER IS IF WE WOULD JUST BE HEALTHY, MENTALLY."

There's no one else in history quite like Frida Kahlo. She was a fierce woman and a curious artist—a revolution in her own right. She was smart, talented, and rebellious in nature. Her art was different, just like her. She painted her struggles and her spirit. Her canvases were steeped in meaning with messages about loss, politics, and defying societal norms.

At a young age growing up in Mexico, Frida was exposed to different views and cultures, beginning with her parents. Her dad was German and her mom was of Spanish and Native Mexican descent. She was raised during the Mexican Revolution, a time when the people of Mexico were fighting to dismantle Mexico's dictatorship. The revolution had such an impact on Frida that she told people for the rest of her life that she was born in 1910, the year the revolution began, three years after her real birth date.

When Frida was six years old, she got polio, a debilitating disease that is highly contagious. It was so severe that she had to stay in her room alone for nine months. The disease affected Frida's right leg, causing it to be much smaller and weaker than her left. This made her walk with a limp and to be teased by other children. Kids wouldn't play with her or talk with her at school. This made her feel lonely as she watched the fun unfold around her.

Frida's doctor recommended she exercise to strengthen her leg. Being naturally coordinated and athletic, she went for it. She boxed, wrestled, played soccer, and swam her way through the loneliness she felt. To avoid further teasing, she began putting layers of socks on the smaller leg to make it

appear thicker. When she got older, she wore long, colorful skirts to hide her difference.

As a teenager, she attended the National Preparatory School in Mexico City to study medicine, with the hopes of becoming a medical illustrator. She was one of only thirty-five girls and among roughly two thousand boys attending the best school in Mexico. It was here where she found a group of friends who were like her. The group called themselves the Cachuchas, named after the peaked hats that they wore. The hats were a sign of rebellion against the rigid dress code of the era.

The members of Frida's crew were known not only for their pranks but also for their intelligence. The friends could often be found debating one another, writing, and devouring books together. The group made up its own language too. It was a great way to be able to say things without getting into trouble.

Frida didn't conform to society's standards. Sometimes she dressed in colorful skirts, and other times, she dressed in boys' clothes. She dated girls and sometimes she dated boys. She didn't care if anyone disapproved because she did what she wanted to do.

When Frida was eighteen, she was in a bus crash that caused her to suffer serious injuries that would haunt her for the rest of her life. Her injuries were so tragic that doctors thought that she'd never walk again. During her many months of recovery at home, she painted her body cast, and when there was no more room on her cast, her parents bought her an easel. She gave some

"THEY THOUGHT I WAS A SURREALIST, BUT I WASN'T, I NEVER PAINTED DREAMS, I PAINTED MY OWN REALITY."

of her first paintings to her friends in the Cachuchas. Her dreams of a good education and career had fallen apart, but new dreams took shape as she gained confidence and courage in painting.

To prove to herself that she had talent, she brought her best paintings to Mexico's most famous artist at the time, Diego Rivera. Diego thought her work was captivating. She didn't just paint what can be seen; she painted the unseen, what is felt on the inside. Her art illustrated her life's experiences in a unique style that distinguished her from other artists of her era and earned her many admirers for generations to come.

Frida had several operations and lived in constant pain as a result of her bus injuries. She loved many different people and married Diego. Her injuries prevented her from having children of her own, which caused her a lot of grief.

She was admired by the world and her own country for expressing her experiences and suffering through art. Frida became the first Latin American woman to have artwork in the Louvre Museum in Paris, where French poet and art critic André Breton described her art as "a ribbon around a bomb."

One of Frida's dreams was to have a solo exhibition in Mexico. It would take many years for this to happen, but she eventually achieved this dream one year before she died. Even though she was so sick, she couldn't miss out on her dream, so she commanded her family to dress her up and bring her to her art show while in bed! And they did!

Frida was only forty-seven years old when she died. Her work still brings a sense of revolution, and she continues to be a treasured artist throughout Mexico and the world.

Mischief, extreme athleticism, hyperactivity, and dismissive teachers sum up Michael Phelps's childhood. He faced many struggles, but his superhero-like mom helped Michael achieve success.

Before Michael became the best swimmer in the world, he was afraid of the pool! He followed his two older sisters to the North Baltimore Aquatic Club in Baltimore, Maryland, where he grew up, when he was seven. Unlike his sisters, he was scared to get his face wet and to swim on his belly for fear he'd sink to the bottom. But Michael had so much extra energy, even after playing multiple sports, that his mom felt that she had to keep him in swimming lessons despite his fears. Luckily, his swim coach was patient with him, and before long, he was so comfortable in the water that he didn't want to get out of the pool!

Michael was a restless kid. He'd climb and jump all over the furniture and other things that weren't meant for climbing. Before fidget toys were around, Michael would play with utensils in his hands to keep them busy during dinner.

He was mischievous. At the pool, he played jokes on other swimmers, like hiding their goggles or stealing their snacks. The swim coaches meant business, though, so if Michael got caught goofing around, he got sent out of the pool and benched.

When Michael was seven, his parents got a divorce. The divorce hurt Michael a lot. He was very close with his mom, but he struggled with his relationship with his dad. Michael's mom meant everything to him. She made sure that he got to every swim practice and meet, and she supported him in school.

In the sixth grade, Michael was diagnosed with attention deficit hyperactivity disorder (ADHD). He had always been hyperactive, which was challenging for teachers. In elementary

school, one teacher told his mom that she could never imagine that he'd ever be able to focus on anything. Michael would prove her and many others wrong.

Little by little, his mom grew to understand his ADHD. He struggled a lot with his attention and impulsivity in school, so she was able to give his teachers and tutors helpful tips to make him more successful.

There were times when ADHD got in the way, though. Sometimes he would forget his swim cap or forget to lace up his swimsuit properly for a meet, and sometimes he'd get distracted and not have enough time to warm up before his races. If he lost a race, he'd throw his goggles, letting his impulsivity win. Eventually, he learned to not only organize himself properly but also to control his impulses in the moment. His mother also developed a cue for Michael

to help with his temper. When she noticed him getting upset, she'd make the letter C with her hand to remind him to "compose" himself, and it worked!

When he was eleven, he advanced in swim groups and was given a new coach, Coach Bob. Michael was terrified of Coach Bob because he was strict and didn't tolerate any goofing around. Coach Bob didn't think he'd be Michael's coach for the long haul. They were complete opposites. But opposites attract, and their partnership would last till the end of Michael's swimming career.

If Michael tried to get out of a workout, Coach Bob would send him home. If he splashed someone in the pool, Coach Bob saw it and let him know. If he skipped part of a workout, Coach Bob wouldn't let him compete until he finished it. To avoid boredom, Coach Bob made Michael's workouts challenging,

"I THINK THAT EVERYTHING IS POSSIBLE AS LONG AS YOU PUT YOUR MIND TO IT. AND YOU PUT THE WORK AND TIME INTO IT. I THINK YOUR MIND REALLY CONTROLS EVERYTHING."

fun, and interesting, and together they found different ways for Michael to improve and reach his goals.

At fifteen years old, Michael competed in his first Olympics in Sydney, Australia. Although he didn't win any medals, he saw how Australia celebrated swimming and became determined to create that same enthusiasm in the United States. Michael went on to compete in four more Olympic Games, earning a total of twenty-eight Olympic medals, twenty-three being gold, in several different events.

There were many moments in between his successes where he struggled. Throughout his career, he suffered with his mental health. He was severely depressed, had problems with substance abuse, and had thoughts of not wanting to live anymore.

Luckily, his thoughts of wanting to live outweighed his sad thoughts. When he realized he needed professional help, he checked himself into a rehabilitation center to heal.

His struggles made him stronger, a better athlete, and a better human. He reached his swimming goals and succeeded in making swimming exciting for fans. His biggest achievement, though, was inspiring others to not be afraid or embarrassed to seek help for their mental health.

Michael retired from swimming in 2016, but he continues to help people through his work with nonprofits that promote active lifestyles, mental health awareness, and water safety. He coaches the next generation of swimmers, is married, and has three children, one of whom is named after his coach!

John Green, who doesn't think he's a very interesting person, is actually a very interesting person to many. John is an author famously known for his uncanny ability to wow readers in the world of young adult fiction. Many of his books are award-winning bestsellers, and some were even turned into blockbuster movies! He has an authentic storytelling style that young people connect to. However, before he could write those stories, John went through quite a bit of struggle.

When he was a kid, bullies targeted John for being awkward, for being himself. He admits that he was perpetually nervous and was also a class clown, but nothing warranted the torture he received. The bullies would stuff him in trash cans or grab each of his limbs and pull on them, stretching him out as if he were a piece of putty!

The experiences were humiliating for him; they made him feel lonely and scared. The worst part was that he didn't know how to make the bullying stop. John dreamed of getting his revenge, but he wasn't a fighter. Instead, he worried and worried about when the bullies would attack next.

Kids were one type of bully John had to deal with. The other was obsessive-compulsive disorder (OCD). OCD can often feel like an invisible bully in your mind, telling you things that aren't true and making you do things that don't make sense.

"I CAN'T NOTICE THE WORLD OUTSIDE OF MYSELF THE WAY THAT I WANT TO

BECAUSE I'M SO DEEPLY AND IRRATIONALLY FOCUSED ON STUFF THAT'S HAPPENING KIND OF WITHIN ME."

John's obsessive thoughts were often out of his control and plagued his daily living. He'd frequently get so stuck in his obsessive thoughts that it was hard for him to think about anything or anyone else, making it challenging for him to be present in his life.

John's social life took a 180-degree turn when he reached high school. He left Orlando, Florida, where he was raised, for Indian Springs School, a boarding school in Alabama. His quirky personality didn't serve him well in middle school, but it gained him many friends in high school. He felt included and found that he wasn't so different from his new friends. Although his social life improved drastically, his grades didn't. He focused on friendships, smoked in plain sight of teachers, and broke a lot of rules. Despite his lack of effort and subpar grades, teachers still wanted to see him succeed. They thought that he was smart and had potential to do great things, so they encouraged and supported him every step of the way.

In college, he double majored in English and religious studies. He was funny and conversational and talked about books like someone would talk about a favorite TV show. He was a great storyteller but was not the best writer yet. John had two positive college professors who challenged him and believed in him. It would take some time for John to write something worthy of publishing, but eventually he'd get there.

Although he wrote stories as a kid and first had the dream of becoming a writer in high school, he didn't know

"I HAVE A REALLY WONDERFUL LIFE. I HAVE A REALLY RICH, FULFILLING LIFE. I ALSO HAVE A PRETTY SERIOUS CHRONIC MENTAL HEALTH PROBLEM. AND THOSE AREN'T MUTUALLY EXCLUSIVE. AND THE TRUTH IS THAT LOTS OF PEOPLE HAVE CHRONIC MENTAL HEALTH PROBLEMS AND STILL HAVE GOOD LIVES."

what kind of writer he'd be. It wasn't until after college when he was working as a chaplain at a children's hospital that he had the idea for what would become his first published book. After three years of edits between John and his mentor, Ilene Cooper, who was also an editor, they felt confident to send it to a publisher. He waited another three months before he got a response—yes!

John's success continued with the publication of five more hugely popular young adult novels, a podcast, and a YouTube channel he hosts with his brother, Hank. Together, they've informed, entertained, and helped a lot of youth get through some of the hard stuff—like dealing with bullies and celebrating differences.

Some days John's OCD is so bad that he can't get off the floor, and other days he can. Running and therapy are tools he uses for his mental health, as well as having a loving and supportive family who's by his side no matter what kind of day it is.

OCD is bossy, anxiety can be crippling, and getting bullied is painful, but the experiences have enhanced John's ability to understand and care for others in a profound way, allowing him to write the stories that so many love.

NORA LUM A.K.A.
AWKWAFINA
ACTRESS + RAPPER
"IT'S GONNA BE OKAY,
AND YOU MAY FEEL LIKE YOU'RE
SUPER WEIRD RIGHT NOW,
BUT LATER IT WILL ALL PAY OFF."

Actress and rapper Nora Lum found her comedic voice at a young age and in an unexpected way—through the loss of her mom. It was devastating for her and everyone around her, but she didn't want people to look at her with sad eyes. Every person around seemed to be crying as they mourned the loss of her mom. Nora understood their sadness, but it was uncomfortable for her, so she decided she'd shift the mood and wipe their tears away by making them laugh.

Her grandma helped Nora's dad raise her in a small one-bedroom apartment in Queens, New York. Although she didn't have the opportunity to grow up with her mother, her grandma became everything she needed to grow into the person she is today.

Nora's grandma, a.k.a. Grammafina, is a symbol of strength, resilience, and individuality. Grammafina not only worked hard to help her son and granddaughter financially, but she also supported Nora in other ways. When kids made fun of her for playing with wrestling figures, being athletic, and wearing sweatsuits, Grammafina encouraged Nora to always be herself.

At the age of seven, Nora was diagnosed with attention deficit hyperactivity disorder (ADHD), which explained her excessive energy and impulsivity, like dunking her face in ice cream for laughs. ADHD didn't deter her. Nora's childhood improvisational escapades spilled into adulthood, keeping her friends and family entertained. But it would be a few more

"DON'T BE ASHAMED OF WHAT MAKES YOU WEIRD BECAUSE THAT IS WHY I LOVE YOU AND THAT'S WHAT MAKES YOU SPECIAL." -GRAMMAFINA

years before the rest of the world would get to enjoy her performances.

In her teenage years, consumed with awkwardness, she put her energy into rapping using the GarageBand program on her computer. Her awkward feelings melted away when she created music. Her friends loved her tracks, so she kept producing more to find what her friends liked and didn't like.

While pursuing her interests, she found solace in the poetry of Charles Bukowski and taught herself the trumpet, gaining her admittance into the famous Fiorello H. LaGuardia High School of Music & Art and Performing Arts. Through her pursuits, she developed an alter ego called Awkwafina. Awkwafina is fearless and confident; Nora is shy and insecure. Awkwafina helps her do the big things that Nora is afraid to do, even to this day.

Throughout her education, Nora wasn't the best student, but she still had the desire to learn. She was accepted to SUNY Albany where she studied

journalism and women's studies. Being raised by a strong woman, her minor in women's studies further informed her feminist ideals.

As an Asian American woman, Awkwafina hardly ever saw movies starring people that looked like her. The only times she did were in films found in the obscure sections of video rental stores. She dreamed of seeing more women and Asians in the performing arts. She looked up to actress and comedian Margaret Cho, and seeing that Margaret was doing what she loved to do made Nora see life's possibilities.

On top of not seeing her culture and people who look like her represented in movies or on TV, Nora struggled with her identity. She didn't completely feel Asian or completely American, and the struggle often left her feeling lonely. But despite her struggles, she kept on making art.

On one life-changing day, she was encouraged to make a music video from one of her tracks. While it was bold and risky for its time, the video became

"I WAS A WEIRD KID."

somewhat of an anthem for women soon after its release. It also got her fired from her nine-to-five job. She hated that job, and getting fired allowed her the freedom to do more of the things that made her happy—such as music.

In the beginning, when she toured solo, people threw tomatoes at her on stage, but she didn't let that stop her. In time, the video that got her fired from her job launched her career. Actor Seth Rogen cast her in one of his movies, which led the way for more. She was afraid of failing and not being good enough. But she pushed through those feelings and kept working hard. Her talent and work ethic showed because each acting opportunity she received turned into another opportunity.

She got a role in *Crazy Rich Asians* and found herself surrounded by other Asian Americans who had faced similar identity struggles and a yearning for cultural representation. Not only did the cast and crew bond over their shared experiences, but the movie also touched many people across the world who felt similarly. Nora and her costars were overjoyed to bring a beautiful romantic comedy that celebrated and represented Asians to people all over the world.

Nora is an example of living outside the box. She doesn't try to fit in, she is simply herself. With support, determination, and talent, this once awkward, laughter-seeking girl with ADHD grew to become a shining star in Hollywood.

President John F. Kennedy marched to his own beat. He didn't conform to rules and expectations and instead defied authority and challenged ideals throughout his life.

John and his eight siblings grew up in Brookline, Massachusetts, with privilege and purpose, being born into one of the richest families in the United States. Their dad, Joe Sr., was a formidable and shrewd businessman with these characteristics seeping into his parenting. The Kennedys weren't followers, they were leaders, sticking together and pushing each other forward.

Every moment was an opportunity to compete and learn. Joe Sr. gave John and his siblings dinner table quizzes on current events, instructed them to write reports on various topics, and promoted fierce competition between them.

Health was a lifelong struggle for John. He was in and out of the hospital for most of his life. As a kid, he had whooping cough, measles, chicken pox, and scarlet fever. He also lived with a mystery illness his entire life, which no doctor or any amount of money could solve. With a family too busy to be with him, John spent his hospital stays alone, taking refuge in books. He never complained about his ailments—instead, he made jokes about them.

John's dad focused on his brother Joe Jr. who got straight As in school, was strong and healthy, and was great at every sport he played. John lived in the shadow of his brother and gave up trying to compete with him. He instead became the class clown. But he was also intellectually curious and had his own subscription to the *New York Times* in high school!

John joined his brother for high school at Choate Rosemary Hall, a boarding school in Connecticut. As John's

"I WAS TWENTY-FOUR BEFORE I KNEW I DIDN'T HAVE TO WIN SOMETHING EVERY DAY."

—EUNICE KENNEDY SCHRIVER, JOHN'S LITTLE SISTER + FOUNDER OF THE SPECIAL OLYMPICS

"I HAVE TWO THINGS TO DO, ONE TO RUN THE SCHOOL, ANOTHER TO RUN JACK [JOHN] KENNEDY AND HIS FRIENDS."
—HEADMASTER GEORGE ST. JOHN

jealousy of his brother grew, a friendship blossomed between John and a boy named Lem, and the two remained close throughout John's life. The friends stayed up late, had messy rooms, and got a thrill out of irritating their teachers.

Nicknamed Public Enemy Number One and Public Enemy Number Two, they led a group of eleven other rebels called The Muckers. The Muckers were notorious for their pranks. One of their biggest was blowing up a toilet!

Despite his untamed behavior, George St. John, the headmaster of Choate, knew that John was smart and that it would take time for him to mature and recognize his own gifts.

History, English, and current local and world affairs were John's main interests and his strongest areas, but he barely survived math, science, and Latin. His grades were uneven, he lived in extreme disorganization, and he rejected the idea of fitting in and following rules.

Even still, through his father's financial and social influence, John first attended Princeton University and then Harvard University for college.

Still suffering from illness, though enjoying the school's social life, John began to take school seriously after a couple of years. He studied international politics and philosophy in Europe and, inspired by his time there, wrote a school paper that was published as "Why England Slept."

After college, John and his brother Joe served in World War II, where John was awarded the Purple Heart and a navy and marine corps medal for courage, endurance, and leadership. Sadly, Joe was killed in a plane crash during a risky private mission. The family was devastated, and the dreams Joe Sr. had for him were destroyed.

John had a growing interest in foreign affairs, and after being urged to join politics by his dad, he decided that he wanted to serve the public. In 1946, John was elected to Congress representing Massachusetts' Eleventh Congressional District. Six years later, he was elected senator of Massachusetts.

In 1960, John ran and won the presidential election! In his inaugural speech, he called for Americans to participate in public service and civil action with his historic words: "Ask not what your country can do for you—ask what you can do for your country." His charm and empathetic nature, as well as his intelligence, stole the hearts of Americans.

Racism was an epidemic that John tried hard to extinguish during his presidency. Black Americans couldn't go to school, eat at restaurants, or sit on a bus with white people. John thought racism and segregation were morally wrong, so he worked hard to dismantle both.

During his presidency, John also prevented a nuclear war, established the Peace Corps, and set a goal for the United States to be the first to put a man on the moon! He wasn't perfect and did make mistakes, but he inspired hope and change in the hearts of many Americans. John's presidency was cut short when he was assassinated while riding in a convertible with his wife, Jackie Kennedy, during a parade in Dallas, Texas. John brought a lot of goodness and love to the world, and he is celebrated as one of the greatest presidents.

GRETA THUNBERG
CLIMATE ACTIVIST
"WHEN HATERS GO AFTER YOUR LOOKS AND DIFFERENCES IT MEANS THEY HAVE NOWHERE LEFT TO GO. AND THEN YOU KNOW YOU'RE WINNING."

Greta Thunberg is a Swedish climate activist who began a climate revolution at the age of fifteen. Her curiosity about the climate began a few years earlier when her class watched a film about the Great Pacific Garbage Patch, a giant collection of trash between California and Hawaii and near Japan. The horror of this collection of litter stuck with Greta. After the film, the rest of her class went about their day as usual, but Greta couldn't stop thinking about the trash. Mother Nature was suffering just as much as she was.

Noticeable signs of Greta's suffering began to appear around age eleven. Up until then, her family had traveled country to country while her mom performed opera. Life was interesting and fun. When a season of performing ended, they'd return to their home in Stockholm. But something began to switch for Greta. She stopped eating and talking, and she seemed to cry more than anything else. Her parents saw her suffering and decided they would stop traveling and help their daughter heal.

Before psychologists could evaluate Greta, she needed to be able to eat. It was a painstakingly slow process that required a lot of patience from the whole family. Greta wanted to eat, but she just couldn't. She had lost so much weight that doctors wanted to admit her into the hospital. She was willing to try to eat more to avoid the hospital, and little by little, she gained weight. As she healed, she spoke about all the bullying she'd experienced at school. Kids pushed her, called her names, and said mean things to her because she acted differently and was quiet. The only place she felt safe was in the school bathroom, but teachers caught on to her hideout and would make her rejoin the rest of the students. Even when her parents complained, the school didn't try to help Greta.

"I HAVE ASPERGER'S SYNDROME AND THAT MEANS I'M SOMETIMES A BIT DIFFERENT FROM THE NORM. AND —GIVEN THE RIGHT CIRCUMSTANCES— BEING DIFFERENT IS A SUPERPOWER."

"THE MOMENT WE DECIDE TO FULFILL SOMETHING WE CAN DO ANYTHING."

The school took sides with the other kids and blamed Greta for getting bullied because she was different.

When she was finally well enough to get an evaluation, Greta was diagnosed with Asperger's syndrome, a form of autism, and OCD. The diagnosis helped her parents understand her needs and the proper support and resources Greta needed to feel safe and successful. The following year, she enrolled in a school that supported neurodiversity in the classroom.

Greta has a photographic memory, allowing her to remember things like the periodic table and the world's capitals. After watching the film about the Great Pacific Garbage Patch, she couldn't get the images and thoughts of Mother Nature suffering out of her mind. She relentlessly researched the ways humans were destroying the earth and what needed to be done to save it. So she made drastic changes to her life, like giving up flying on airplanes, inspiring her parents to get an electric car and install solar panels on their home, and eating plants instead of animals.

Her intense single interest with climate change may seem different to people, but being an autistic young person with OCD has given Greta the strength, determination, and intense interest to inform the whole world on a global problem that adults have yet to slow, stop, or reverse.

Greta wants to help heal the world. She's eaten lunch with scientists and people in Greenpeace. She influenced publishers to rewrite textbooks to present the scientific facts, and she won first prize in a writing competition about climate change.

In August 2018, Greta decided that she would go on a school strike for three weeks leading up to the parliamentary election in Sweden. She made flyers, signs, and posted on her social media accounts. From day one of her school strike, she spoke to reporters and ate her bean pasta on the Parliament steps—which completely shocked her parents because eating in public was far outside of her comfort zone. Each day, she was joined by other children, adults, and classes on field trips. The attention brought her to tears because it was the first time that kids weren't mean to her.

On the last day of the school strike, Greta was surrounded by a thousand people in front of parliament. When the day was over, she wasn't satisfied. So the very next day, she spoke at the People's Climate March in Stockholm where she announced that she would strike every Friday for the climate, for the future. This turned into the worldwide movement, Fridays for Future, where students around the world didn't attend school but instead gathered in their city streets and protested to save the environment. They hoped that politicians would listen to them and make the necessary changes that the climate crisis needs. Kids can't vote, but they can take action!

Greta still leads climate strikes, and has been nominated for the Nobel Peace Prize two years in a row, inspiring more people to care about the environment than she ever imagined. Greta continues to challenge people to think about the climate crisis and make their own changes to help the environment.

SKOLSTREJK för KLIMATET

SCHOOL STRIKE for the CLIMATE

"WE SHOWED THAT WE ARE UNITED, AND THAT WE, YOUNG PEOPLE, ARE UNSTOPPABLE."

Bobby Herrera grew up with the determination to prove himself to anyone and everyone around him, just like his dad grew up with the audacity to change his family's status of poverty and misfortune.

During World War II, the United States and Mexico made a historical agreement that brought laborers from Mexico to the States. The United States needed workers to maintain its farming industry while Americans were fighting overseas, and Mexico wanted to contribute to the Allies of World War II. The agreement was called the Bracero Program, meaning "one who works with his arms," and it helped both countries. In fact, the agricultural success of the United States has been built and sustained by the hands of migrant farm workers. Bobby's dad was one of those workers and was happy to be a part of it.

When the program ended, Bobby's dad was allowed to stay in the United States and bring his family. So Bobby's family moved and became a migrant farm—working family. Every year from April through September, his family would leave their home in New Mexico to work in onion, potato, pear, and sugar beet fields. Year after year, they traveled to Colorado, Wyoming, and Idaho, leaving school before it ended and arriving back after it had begun.

Wyoming was Bobby's favorite! It was the only place where he felt like he and his family were on a vacation because his parents would treat the family to an A&W drive-in dinner and enjoy hamburgers and other treats. In those brief moments, it felt

"EVERYONE NEEDS TO BE SEEN."

like he and his family's work paid off and they had finally "made it."

Back home in their two-bedroom, one-bathroom house that he shared with his parents and twelve brothers and sisters, Bobby felt invisible. He was the eleventh child and the first to be born in the United States. English was not his family's native language, so he didn't understand or learn how to speak English until elementary school. From sunrise till sunset, with school sandwiched in the middle, he'd work in the cotton fields. He and his family's work was important, but he realized they were different from the families surrounding them. Theirs and other migrant farmer's work filled the plates of families across the country. However, no one recognized their role as important. As a family, they spent half the year away from home working, missing out on school, and connecting with friends, without anyone being aware of their efforts.

Even though they worked long, hard hours farming crops, they didn't make a lot of money. Bobby recognized that his family used food stamps, and he and his siblings benefited from the free school lunch program. He felt like he had to protect his family from the judgments of others, so he'd wait for the grocery store to be empty before going in to pick up groceries using the food stamps. And, in school, he'd distract his friends with jokes to keep them from seeing the lunch worker check off his name from the free lunch program list.

Bobby also struggled with bottled-up anger for most of his young life, and that anger overwhelmed him and got him into fistfights. He was also an extremely competitive kid. If someone told him he couldn't do something, he'd prove them wrong. Bobby had a lot of energy, so he played several sports throughout his childhood, but football became a great outlet for his anger, energy, and frustration.

In his junior year of high school, Bobby had a life-changing moment that would shift his outlook on life. After basketball games, he and his brother Ed would always eat their mom's homemade

"EVERYONE DESERVES THE OPPORTUNITY TO SUCCEED."

burritos on the team bus while the rest of their teammates would get a postgame dinner together. They didn't have the money to eat with their team. After one basketball game, a dad of a teammate, who was a successful businessman, stepped back onto the bus to talk to the brothers. He expressed that it would make him happy to pay for their dinners so they could be with their team. The only thanks he needed was for them to give back to someone else one day.

Bobby felt this kindness in such a way that it ended up changing him. An adult saw him as a person and treated him with respect and trusted him to pay the generosity forward. Bobby suddenly realized that he could do anything he wanted with his life. He could be someone and make a difference.

Although his childhood was different and challenging, it prepared Bobby for his future. After high school, Bobby served in the US Army. The long hours and physical demands of bootcamp felt similar to the work he'd been doing his whole life. While his comrades were struggling to keep up, Bobby found it easy and earned the highest honor in basic training—Distinguished Honor Graduate.

After the army, Bobby started his own company, Populus Group, which connects people to jobs and works to improve the lives of veterans and kids across the country. Through his work, he encourages collaboration, honesty, and original thinking, and he found a way to make a difference giving people opportunities to succeed.

TREVOR NOAH

COMEDIAN + TV PERSONALITY

"WHEN YOU ARE HONEST IN YOUR COMEDY, YOU HAVE TO ACKNOWLEDGE THE WORLD THAT YOU ARE IN. THROUGH A COMEDIC VOICE YOU'RE TALKING ABOUT WHAT NEEDS TO BE TALKED ABOUT, WHETHER IT'S RACE RELATIONS OR POLITICS OR ANYTHING THAT'S HAPPENING ON A GLOBAL SCALE OR AN AMERICAN SCALE, THAT'S EXACTLY THE SPACE *THE DAILY SHOW* IS IN."

Trevor Noah is a stand-up comedian and was the host of a satirical news show on Comedy Central. But before he was a household name, he was just another kid growing up in South Africa seeking out friendship and acceptance in a society that separated people by color, race, and tribe. He questioned the rules and laws in place in his country and often defied authority, while bringing mischief along with him.

His primary school years were spent in a strict Catholic school full of rules that Trevor loved to question and find loopholes for. Goofing around and playing pranks were thrilling to him. Often this resulted in disciplinary action, like getting his mouth washed out with soap. Nothing anyone did to Noah deterred him from his antics, though. One time, he released the contents of a fire extinguisher into a piano before a big school performance. During the performance, foam exploded out of the piano!

His school sent him to a psychologist three times because his behavior was so disruptive, but each time, the psychologist would report that the school was just too strict for a creative kid like Trevor. However, as an adult Trevor was diagnosed with attention deficit hyperactivity disorder (ADHD) and depression. Therapy, having a routine, and setting goals for himself have helped him manage his mental wellness. Before his diagnosis and any adult's understanding of how his brain worked, he spent a lot of school time in detention!

"TREVOR IS SO NAUGHTY. HE'S THE NAUGHTIEST CHILD I'VE EVER COME ACROSS IN MY LIFE."
—TREVOR'S GRANDMA

Trevor was born during apartheid—South Africa's rule of extremism toward people of color. Although Black people were the majority, white people were in control and considered themselves superior. One major law was that Black people were not allowed to associate with white people. People who broke this law could go to jail. Trevor's mom broke that law. She met a white man who she really enjoyed spending time with, and together, they had Trevor.

Trevor was born with lighter skin, and because his mom was not supposed to be with a white man, she lied on his birth certificate, saying that Trevor was from another country. If the authorities had known the truth or investigated her, she could've been sent to jail and Trevor would've been taken away from her.

In his early childhood, he had to be hidden. Because his mom was Black and his skin was lighter, she hired women who looked more like Trevor to take him to the park, and she'd act as the servant to these women. They lived in constant fear that the government would take him away, and there were snitches who would be rewarded by turning in those who broke the law. Because Trevor had to hide so much, he spent a lot of time alone reading books and escaping into his imagination.

South Africa's unfair class structure forced certain people into places with no hope of getting out. Most kids in Trevor's neighborhood never saw anything beyond it. That didn't stop his mom, though. She tried to show Trevor that there was a big, wide world outside of their neighborhood. She drove him through fancy neighborhoods and took him to drive-in movies and ice-skating!

As apartheid was gradually being dismantled, the company Trevor's mom worked for offered scholarships to families in need. The scholarship program helped Trevor attend the

"I ALWAYS FELT AN INNATE JOY MAKING PEOPLE LAUGH. I ALWAYS LOVED PERFORMING. AND THEN SOMEBODY PAID ME TO DO IT AS A PROFESSION."

Catholic school he eventually disrupted so much. Despite its rules, it was diverse and wasn't segregated. All the students dressed the same, ate together, read the same books, and had the same teachers no matter their race.

After school, Trevor had to find unique ways to navigate racial discrimination. He learned from his mom at an early age that even if you looked different from someone, you could still connect with them if you could communicate with them. Trevor learned to speak as many languages as he could to be able to move in and out of different groups of people.

His life changed one day after his cousin took him to a comedy club. The comedians on stage were funny, but Trevor's cousin insisted that Trevor was funnier. Before he knew it, Trevor was on stage telling stories. The crowd went wild, and Trevor quickly moved forward with his newly revealed gift.

Trevor worked all hours, doing multiple comedy gigs a night. He turned his life's stories into comedy, and people loved it. He toured all over South Africa and became the first South African to do stand-up on late-night TV in the United States. Although he was a star in South Africa, he had trouble making it in America. Then one day Jon Stewart, host of Comedy Central's *The Daily Show*, saw a recording of Trevor and said, "Yep, that guy's going to take my chair one day."

In 2015, Jon Stewart's prediction came true. Trevor Noah took over the *The Daily Show* for nearly eight years, and he continues to do stand-up comedy, enlightening and entertaining crowds all over the world. Trevor pulls much of his comedy from his experience with race and politics and uses his popularity to not only shed light on the struggles of underserved people around the world, but also to help them through the Trevor Noah Foundation.

HAMISH BREWER
EDUCATOR + PRINCIPAL + AUTHOR
"YOU SHOW ME A KID THAT CAN'T LEARN, I'VE JUST MET A TEACHER THAT GAVE UP ON 'EM."

Hamish Brewer's appetite to keep kids interested in school is enormous. Mainly because when he was in school, he wasn't inspired and learning didn't come easy for him. School brought him a lot of sadness and anxiety. He also had challenges at home, which made life even harder. As an educator and principal, he knows there are a lot of kids who are growing up with similar struggles as his, so he has made it his mission to do what he can to help lead kids to success.

He grew up in New Zealand, where he'd often play sports, skateboard with friends, or watch professional skateboarders on TV, wishing he could be one of them. But his childhood was very different from other kids he knew. Hamish's mom left his family when he was a teenager, and his dad was an alcoholic. His family was also poor and almost lost their house several times because they couldn't pay their bills, but his dad showed them love and tried the best he could.

Hamish spent his childhood pretending he was confident, but he really wasn't. However, he created a space that gave him a sliver of hope. On the walls of his bedroom garage, he hung up a world map and put pins in the places he hoped to go one day. Along with the map were pictures of different places around the world that ignited his hopes and dreams. He had a gut feeling that he wanted to make a difference in people's lives, but he wasn't sure how he could.

He failed his exams in his last year of high school and was forced to repeat an entire year of school. At first, he felt lost, but then he knew that he could either wallow in his sadness or make a change. He chose to make a change.

Hamish flipped his mindset to live with passion and develop strong and positive relationships. He calls this being "relentless." Even when he was told he wasn't smart enough to be a teacher, he ignored the comments and continued to go after his dreams. He applied to a teacher's college in New Zealand and

"I HAVE BEEN FIGHTING AGAINST RULES, REGULATIONS, AND SOCIETAL NORMS SINCE ABOUT THE TIME I LEARNED TO WALK. FOR ME, THE FREEDOM TO EXPRESS ONE'S OPINIONS AND INDIVIDUALITY IS PART OF WHAT IT MEANS TO LIVE A PURPOSEFUL, PASSIONATE, AND INTENTIONAL LIFE."

relied on his exceptional communication skills in his interview. He was accepted into the program and carried the idea of being relentless through college and into his career. Today, Hamish is now known as the "relentless, tattooed, skateboarding principal."

From the get-go, Hamish taught his students from a place of love, because love was something that was missing from his own education. He made school fun and interesting, like having students make their own costumes, put on fashion shows, or turn classrooms into castles during medieval studies. His goal was to give kids the educational experience that he wished he'd had.

After five years of teaching in New Zealand, Hamish needed a break. He'd dreamed of traveling his entire childhood and decided it was time. He backpacked alone and free, exploring Australia and Thailand. With space to reflect on his past, he was able to grow for his future.

When it was time to get back to work, he joined the Visiting International Faculty program, which landed him in Virginia. And ever since his arrival, he's been disrupting the US educational system in the best way possible. His love and enthusiasm for education has led neglected schools to success.

Hamish is decorated in tattoos, or ta moko, which represent his New Zealand Maori ancestry and show the story of his life. He has a boisterous, infectious presence as he rides his skateboard down the school hallways greeting kids as they head to their classes. At the two Virginia schools where he's been principal, he painted the walls with inspiring quotes, like "Leave no one behind," and pictures of influential figures, such as Martin Luther King Jr., Frida Kahlo, and President Obama. Each word and drawing helps light the way for students to dream, be inspired, and do their best.

"RELATIONSHIPS ARE THE MOST IMPORTANT COMPONENT IN ENGAGING, INSPIRING, AND MOTIVATING OUR STUDENTS."

Skateboarding wasn't always considered a positive outlet for kids because it wasn't a traditional sport, but for Hamish, it was a big part of his identity and still is to this day. So he created Mr. Brewer's Skateboard Giveaway, which allows him to share his favorite sport by rewarding hardworking students with a skateboard! The program has put a spotlight not only on skateboarding but also shows kids that hard work pays off.

Hamish's energy infiltrates any space he occupies, inspiring and strengthening not just his school community but teachers all over the country through his book, *Relentless: Changing Lives by Disrupting the Educational Norm*, numerous lectures, and appearances in the media. Hamish has won awards, been recognized as principal of the year, and has also turned two schools around. His hope as a principal is not just to educate kids but to bring the community together like a giant family and to provide students with the best possible learning environment for success. Students and teachers alike can feel how big his heart is.

Clay Marzo is out of place on land, but perfectly in his place in the ocean. He intuitively bends in any direction on his surfboard to ride the waves the ocean releases. He can visualize what each wave feels and looks like, which helps him to predict how to ride them. And he has the uncanny ability to remember every single wave he's ever surfed!

Clay senses ocean waves like no one else, and as long as there are no crowds in the water, he will miss meals to spend the entire day in the ocean. His focus remains on the ocean and catching the best waves while everything else spills off his radar.

As a baby, Clay loved bath time, and it was also one of the only things that calmed him down. He was born on the Hawaiian island of Maui, three weeks past his due date. He received low scores on the test given to newborns, known as the Apgar test, which assesses the health of a baby, but his doctors were not alarmed. His mom worried about whether those scores would mean health issues for Clay in the future.

Clay began swim lessons at two weeks old, and after only a few weeks, he was swimming underwater! At seven months old, he began walking and showing his independence. By nine months, he could swim the length of the pool. His older brother and younger sister could do the same, but Clay's instinctual nature in the water would prove to be very different from his siblings.

Clay studied his older brother, Cheyne's, surfing from the shore in between moments of collecting seashells and playing in the sand. By the time Clay turned one, he was riding on the front of his dad's surfboard—which freaked

"GIVE ME AN OCEAN AND SOME WAVES... AND I WILL PAY ATTENTION ALL THE TIME."

people out, but Clay loved it and showed no fear.

At the age of two, he was already boogie boarding by himself in any type of wave. He knew when to dive in and when to pop up. He wasn't scared of the ocean at all. In fact, it was almost like he and the ocean shared a secret language.

When Clay gets excited, he rapidly and excitedly rubs his hands together or claps enthusiastically and throws his arms in the air. This reaction is usually related to surfing, and any surfer who knows Clay knows this behavior well.

Unlike his clear talent and interest in surfing, school was a challenge for him. He disrupted the class by talking, not finishing his work, drawing, and daydreaming about being in the water. He'd stare off into space and picture himself riding the waves, sometimes moving his hand in the air like he was

surfing. Teachers were frustrated with him and would complain that he was different and slow to learn, and they suggested he had a learning challenge.

Over the years, his mom considered that maybe he had OCD or ADHD, but those conclusions didn't feel completely right. She was tired of spending so much time meeting with teachers, principals, and psychologists. His parents just wanted him to be a normal kid, to conform like all the other kids—to be quiet, sit still, and do his work. That wasn't Clay, though.

He was overwhelmed by the number of kids, loud noises, and mostly mean teachers at school. He struggled with understanding people and knowing how to respond correctly. His responses were often awkward and harsh, unintentionally hurting others' feelings. Socializing was challenging and confusing for him.

Clay became a professional surfer at the age of eleven. With a busy travel schedule and mounting school issues, his mom decided to homeschool him. She quickly realized the difficulty his teachers had. The typical techniques used to help kids grow and learn didn't work for Clay, and his behavior continued to be an unsolved puzzle.

Quiksilver was one of his surfing sponsors. They paid him to surf and promote their brand, and when they realized Clay couldn't behave normally around people, they asked for a diagnosis to explain his behavior or they were going to fire him.

With some hesitation, Clay went to see a doctor that specialized in neurodevelopmental disorders. After a few days of tests, Clay was diagnosed with Asperger's syndrome, a form of autism that, among other things, is characterized by difficulty with social interaction and nonverbal communication, as well as having restricted interests and distinctive strengths. He and his family were relieved to have an answer. They were soon equipped with the understanding and resources to support Clay in his life.

With Clay's diagnosis, the surfing world could work with him in a way that was more mutually beneficial. He is able to create the surfing experiences and schedules that work best for him and his mental health. He loves music, needs the ocean, and is still considered to be one of the best surfers in the world!

"WAVES ARE HOME TO ME."

Joe Grand, also known by his hacker name Kingpin, has been hacking since he was seven years old. Building, taking apart, and modifying electronics was a natural talent of his. He never thought it would become his lifestyle; it was just something he enjoyed.

Joe came into the world ready to challenge society. He grew up in Boston, Massachusetts, a city known for its rebellion and fierce phenoms in sports, medicine, and politics. Perhaps it was the history that lined the streets, the ghosts of boundary pushers that came before him, or maybe it was just the way he was made, but whatever it was, Joe was always toeing the line of curiosity and mischief.

In kindergarten, he was sent to the timeout box for misbehaving. Little did teachers know that he'd meet his lifelong best friend, Josh Fernandez, in that same box. The two became inseparable mischief-makers.

Neither of them can remember why they were sent to the principal's office so often or why teachers picked on them. But outside of school, they can remember tormenting the Boston train drivers. They had a skeleton key they'd use to sneak into the closed areas of the train. They'd honk the horn and say funny things through the PA system. To avoid getting caught, they'd jump out of the window and run away! Joe was impulsive and lived in the moment without thinking about the consequences of his actions.

Throughout elementary school, Joe was a chubby kid who wore thick brown glasses and bulky sweatpants. If he wasn't slouched over his computer, he was skateboarding around the city streets, pausing to eat donuts, flirt with ballerinas from the Boston Ballet School summer program, or harass tourists who crossed his path. When other kids were listening to Top 40 pop music, Joe was listening to punk and hard-core music like the Misfits and Youth of Today. Skateboarding, music, and his curiosity about computers were drastically different from what most other kids were into.

He was bullied by his family and kids at school. He used to joyfully sing around his house until his brother and sister made fun of him so much that he stopped singing completely. Classmates made up a song about him called "Joey is a Piggy." He was called a "scrub" for what he looked like and a "nerd" for his love of computers. This caused Joe to develop a chip on his shoulder, a lack of self-esteem, and an attitude of: "It's me against the world!"

His hacker mentality grew quite innocently—exploring bulletin board systems (an early way for people to talk to each other over the computer) and making electronic gadgets, like a "universal garage door opener" that could open any garage door in his neighborhood! Being a hacker made him feel like he had a superpower—having the skills to do things that other kids couldn't do.

Joe would stay out all night dumpster diving for equipment that could be salvaged and looking for computer passwords and credit card receipts. He'd use the credit card receipts to go shopping, even renting limos for him and his friends to ride around in.

All of this felt normal to him—that is, until he got arrested. Joe was a sophomore in high school and in a hacker group with other mischievous kids from around the country. During winter break, Joe's parents let him fly out to a fellow hacker's home in Michigan. They decided to break into a telephone company hoping to steal equipment that would help them hack into the phone network. The plan didn't work. They were all arrested. But he got lucky. He was the only one that was under the age of eighteen. Though he wasn't sent to juvenile hall (jail for

"IT'S ME AGAINST THE WORLD!"

"YOU HAVE TO BE DEDICATED. YOU GOTTA PUT IN THE WORK FOR WHAT YOU BELIEVE IN AND WHAT YOU'RE DOING. IT'S NOT GOING TO COME EASY. IF YOU'RE SEARCHING FOR INSTANT GRATIFICATION, YOU AREN'T GOING TO GET IT. YOU GET TO WHERE YOU WANT TO GO BY WORKING HARD AND DOING WHAT YOU LOVE."

U.S. CONGRESS

TAN KING PIN MUDGE WELD POND SPACE ROGUE

kids), his parents demanded that he get a job or take up a sport to keep him out of more trouble. He knows that if his skin color or socioeconomic status were different, his life might not have turned out the way it did.

Joe chose to join the cross-country team. Not because he had any natural talent for running but because he had a few friends on the team and thought it would be fun to hang out with them. He got off to a rough start, dry heaving and passing out, but he stuck with it. Running helped his body and mind feel better, and he even got good at the sport.

After his run-in with the law, he was soon invited to be a part of another hacker group that explored computers and networks, but legally. L0pht Heavy Industries was like a clubhouse. The other hackers in the group were older than Joe and became his mentors, teaching him the importance of sharing information,

empowering others, and using his skills for good. In 1998, the L0pht had the opportunity to testify in front of the US Congress about what hackers can do and even started one of the first cybersecurity consulting companies!

Even though Joe felt out of step with society and still harbored anger from his experiences as a kid, he went on to become a professional hacker and computer engineer. He was a cohost of a TV show called *Prototype This!* on the Discovery Channel and received an honorary doctorate from the University of Advancing Technology. He later discovered meditation, which allowed him to accept his past and be grateful for his experiences and gifts. When Joe isn't with his wife, two kids, and dog, he's teaching all over the world, creating YouTube videos about engineering and hacking, and running up mountains and through forests.

JONATHAN VAN NESS

HAIR STYLIST + TV PERSONALITY

"MY PHILOSOPHY WAS VERY MUCH TO EMBRACE YOURSELF AND LOVE WHAT YOU ARE. INSTEAD OF MAKING YOU SOMETHING YOU'RE NOT."

Jonathan Van Ness's heart is big and his joy is contagious. His care for people, laughter, and beauty products are just a few of the things that make him special. Now known as JVN, he felt like the odd one out through most of his childhood, living in the small Midwestern town of Quincy, Illinois. It took him a long time to get to a place where he accepted and loved every part of himself. But once he had those key ingredients, his life became more vibrant than ever.

JVN grew up with two brothers who were very different from him. They didn't like any of the same things as he did. JVN was a boy who didn't like traditional "boy sports," a boy who liked dressing up in girl's clothes, and a boy who liked boys. He seemed to be too different and being different wasn't completely accepted, which often made his childhood feel lonely and confusing.

When JVN's brothers went off to soccer practices, he stayed home to watch his favorite TV programs—women's gymnastics and figure skating. He was enthralled! He wanted to be as graceful and powerful as the women athletes he idolized. So he spent many afternoons practicing and performing his self-choreographed gymnastics routines nonstop for his family!

JVN wore traditional boys' clothes but felt equally comfortable in makeup and dresses. His dad didn't understand him and disapproved of the way he was expressing himself. However, he felt safe

"GOING TO SCHOOL WAS AN ABSOLUTE TERROR FOR ME, FOR, LIKE, A DECADE."

around his mom, and she gave him the freedom to express himself in dresses, tights, and makeup!

Junk food, especially sweet treats, were JVN's go-to. He loved food and loved eating a lot of it. Food soothed him and brought him joy because most of the time he felt sad. But all the food that he craved and consumed made him feel worse about himself.

After church on Sundays, families would take turns going to each other's houses. An older boy would often bring JVN into a closet to play doctor. But the older boy was not playing doctor with him. He was touching him in places he shouldn't be. Four-year-old JVN felt confused. Good feelings and scary feelings were all mixed up inside of him. The first time he tried to tell his mom, he was little and couldn't explain the experience well. And the uncomfortable feelings

remained inside of him, causing him to disrupt and misbehave both at home and at school.

JVN began to rebel against his parents. He fought with his mom a lot, and she eventually recommended he talk to a therapist. As he sat with the therapist, he talked about his life, and in doing so, the therapist was able to identify the scary and confusing experience JVN had when he was four. It was called sexual abuse and it wasn't OK. It is damaging in many ways when someone's body is harmed, and the healing process is different for everyone. JVN and his family had a difficult time healing from the experience, but over time, they did.

In high school, JVN wanted to become his school's first male cheerleader. But before he could try out, he had to get in shape. He hired a coach and worked tirelessly. His efforts paid off

"I WAS THE FIRST MALE CHEERLEADER OF MY HIGH SCHOOL. IT'S VERY HARD TO EMBARRASS ME — IT TAKES A LOT."

because he got strong, learned how to do flips, and made the varsity team!

JVN began to feel as though he was outgrowing his small town, and he wanted new experiences. So he graduated high school early by taking the GED and moved out of the house. College wasn't a good fit for him, but cosmetology school was. Once he settled into his new career, there was no turning back. He loved being with people and making them feel beautiful, even when he struggled with his own sadness. JVN suffered from depression, which would lead him to use drugs to feel good. Though drugs never cured his depression, therapy, rehabilitation centers, and practicing yoga did. And when he was diagnosed with AIDS, a life-long virus that can be managed with medicine, he finally felt the urgent need to change his life for the better.

Through therapy, yoga, nutrition, and exercise, JVN was able to maintain his wellness and pursue his dreams. After starting a podcast and auditioning for different projects, JVN auditioned for the TV series *Queer Eye*. Hundreds of gay men with various skills and expertise auditioned for the show. JVN didn't think he stood a chance, but to his surprise, he was chosen to be one of the five costars! Within a few years, he expanded his quest to bring healing, joy, and laughter with his stand-up comedy tour, Getting Curious, and other great projects.

JVN has thrived not only because he loves his work and helping people feel good about themselves, but because he loves himself. He understands sadness, loneliness, and feeling different and encourages people to seek support if they feel those things. Even though life was hard at times, he figured out how to make life better for himself. Now he is not only able to live his dreams, he is able to help others live theirs!

"I HAD TO FIGHT, A LOT OF YEARS, TO BE REALLY PROUD OF THIS PERSON I SEE IN THE MIRROR AND TO REALLY LOVE THIS PERSON."

SEANE CORN
YOGA TEACHER + ACTIVIST
"BREATHE, AND EVERYTHING CHANGES.
FIND THE BREATH AND YOU FIND THE MIND."

eane Corn's smile lights up any room. She has a big heart, a strong voice, and a gift for teaching yoga, which she's done for more than twenty-five years! She believes that yoga is activism, and she has been a leader in inspiring yoga teachers and students around the world to bring awareness and social change to issues and communities that have been underserved and overlooked.

Her childhood was spent in a small town in New Jersey with her family. Although life may have looked easy for her from the outside, on the inside, Seane had silent struggles. And these silent struggles ended up shaping her future.

With two rambunctious brothers always urging her to do some crazy shenanigan, Seane often forced herself to keep up with them even though she really didn't want to. Fear would pulse through her body with every stunt they urged her to do. Of course, she didn't want to be the odd one out, so she'd always cave and do whatever antic they prodded her to do.

Her young parents weren't particularly empathetic. They celebrated toughness. If Seane didn't cry when she got hurt, that made her parents proud. Talking about feelings and emotions wasn't their strength, which was a problem because Seane had a lot of feelings inside of her. It became more problematic for Seane when a relative sexually abused her when she was six years old, breaching her personal space and safety. It was a childhood trauma too big for her to handle on her own. Even though her family dealt with this traumatic event, no one in her family helped her understand and process what happened to her. She felt shame and embarrassment, and she wasn't given the opportunity to cry or to be mad about it. Instead, she hid the emotions she felt.

"STAY WITH THIS, SEANE. BREATHE INTO THIS. DON'T RUN, PLEASE! WHAT DOES YOUR BODY WANT TO SAY?"

Because of the lack of control she had during her traumatic experience, Seane developed anxiety and obsessive-compulsive disorder (OCD). Seane felt like she had control over her body, but in reality, OCD was in control. Whenever she felt the rise of anxiety and obsessive thoughts, her compulsion would be to do things in fours and eights. If someone tapped her shoulder once, she'd find creative ways to get them to tap it three more times. OCD told her that if she didn't get her shoulder tapped four or eight times, then something bad would happen to her or someone she knew. This is not true, but OCD is a trickster.

Seane didn't know that what she needed to do was to say no to OCD and breathe through the discomfort until the feeling went away. OCD is powerless when it's ignored.

Although her trauma was hiding inside of her, her life wasn't so bad. At school, she was popular, pretty, and athletic. Her blue eyes, long curly blond hair, and warm smile coexisted with a ton of confidence. Grades were a different story, though. She wasn't very good at school. Things would get overwhelming, and she'd just give up. She learned very differently, and she grew up in a generation where learning differences weren't supported.

In high school, she had an English teacher who taught to her unique abilities instead of letting her fall through the cracks. This teacher assigned Seane different books to read and then had her write about how those books made her feel. For the first time,

Seane's gift of understanding others was being supported.

After high school, Seane went to New York City. In the big city, she worked a variety of jobs, learned valuable lessons, and discovered yoga. There, she met her friend Billy, who taught her that beauty and love surround everyone despite their circumstances. She holds and applies this philosophy to her own yoga teaching and practice to this day.

Seane's yoga practice deepened, and she began seeing a therapist to help with her anxiety and childhood trauma. OCD was still a nagging pain in her life, but yoga brought her the breakthroughs she needed. In one yoga class, a teacher instructed the class to breathe through the discomfort. Little did he know, it was exactly what she needed to hear, as she was trying to carry out a compulsion in that exact moment.

Throughout the years, Seane has continued to heal and grow and has dedicated her life to teaching yoga and guiding people in spiritual wellness all over the world. She's been named National Yoga Ambassador for YouthAIDS, awarded the Global Green Millennium Award, and honored by the Smithsonian Institute for her relentless work in yoga and activism. She was a cofounder of Off the Mat Into the World, a collective of yoga practitioners who bring activism, healing, and positive change to people and communities all over the world. Through her own yoga practice and teaching, Seane continues to spread love, kindness, and healing.

"YOGA SIMPLY SAYS PAY ATTENTION TO WHAT'S HAPPENING, AS IT'S HAPPENING, AND NOTICE YOUR REACTION TO IT."

TARIQ TROTTER A.K.A. BLACK THOUGHT

RAPPER + ARTIST

"FOR ME, THE ARTS HAS ALWAYS BEEN SORT OF MY SAVING GRACE."

Black Thought, MC for legendary hip-hop group The Roots, has been rap battling and freestyling since he was a kid. In 2016, he was interviewed by Harvard Innovation Lab for their speaker series, *The Other Side*. When they asked him if he could freestyle for them, he lit up, and with the stroke of his beard and a thoughtful pause, he sat up in his seat and delivered a rhythmic, insightful performance like no one else. The people in the room applauded in awe as they witnessed a master at his craft.

Tariq Trotter grew up in the Germantown neighborhood of Philadelphia. There were many experiences, both good and bad, that influenced him. His dad was killed when he was only one year old, so his mom and grandma raised him. His parents were a part of the Nation of Islam, and his grandma was Christian. He grew up reading both the Koran, the sacred book of Islam, and the Bible.

Tariq was born an artist. Not a day went by that he wasn't walking around town with his art supplies stuffed into his backpack. When all his friends went to the park to play, he would sit down to draw. He loved reading and soon developed an appetite for history, science, and English. While riding in the back seat of his family's car, he listened intently to the public news radio playing over the airwaves. His neighborhood streets offered a different type of education. Some lessons were good, some were scary and dangerous.

"[SCRUB TIME] ONLY ADDED TO MY LOVE AND APPRECIATION FOR THE ARTS

BUT IT ALSO GAVE ME A DEEPER APPRECIATION FOR MY NEIGHBORHOOD AND THE BEAUTIFICATION OF WHERE WE LIVE. I WANTED TO BEAUTIFY AND VANDALIZE LESS."

Tariq saw a lot of things that kids shouldn't have to see, which caused him a lot of emotional stress throughout the years. In adulthood, he learned that the stress and pain he felt his whole life was post-traumatic stress disorder (PTSD), a disorder that may occur in people who have experienced or witnessed a traumatic event. For years, he struggled with his mental health, but music and visual art helped him move forward.

Around the age of twelve, Tariq swapped out his color pencils for spray paint and the city streets became his canvas. Street graffiti was illegal and doing it ultimately got him arrested. His consequence was to do "scrub time" to clean up the city's graffiti. He was supervised by a woman named Jane Golden, and today, Jane and Tariq work together for the Mural Arts Philadelphia program.

Despite his mischief, Tariq was accepted into Philadelphia's High School for Creative and Performing Arts (CAPA) for visual art. History and English were his favorite classes, and he considered becoming an architect, illustrator, or painter. Tariq loved the rhythm of Shakespeare, particularly the use of iambic pentameter. Rappers like Big Daddy Kane, Kool G Rap, and Rakim were not only rapping in iambic pentameter, but they were also hugely influential in hip-hop and rap's powerful surge in the music world. Tariq was learning from them as well as local Philadelphia rapper, Schoolly D, during this pivotal time in music history.

At CAPA, Tariq met Ahmir "Questlove" Thompson, who would become his lifelong friend and band cofounder. They met in the principal's office—Tariq was in trouble and Questlove was not. The opposites attracted, and they became instant friends. The two formed a duo called The Square Roots and performed on the streets with their drum kit, upright bass, and Tariq's raps. They made some good money and demolished the talent show circuit. But Tariq got into fights, skipped classes, and eventually was kicked out of high school. Tariq was also selling drugs and was heading in the wrong direction. His grandma was worried, so she sent Tariq to live with his uncle in Detroit until he was able to turn his life around.

When Tariq felt ready to return to Philadelphia, he came home to tragedy. His mom had been killed. He was sad and angry, but instead of letting his anger control him, he turned to his music.

All of Tariq's experiences have become a part of his growth and understanding of the world and, in turn, have informed his thoughts and his music. Over his musical journey, Tariq has gone by different names—DT Rock, Double T, and finally Black Thought. The band he started with Questlove, The Square Roots, became The Roots, a "hip-hop/neo-soul band" that has toured all over the world, won Grammy Awards, and is the house band for the *Tonight Show Starring Jimmy Fallon*! He has become a respected and prominent artist in music, works with a health and wellness nonprofit, and flexes his natural-born entrepreneurial spirit in the fashion, TV, and movie industries.

"EVERYTHING WE'VE EVER DONE HAS BEEN FOR ARTISTRY'S SAKE AND FOR THE GREATER GOOD, AND PAYING HOMAGE TO THOSE WHO CAME BEFORE US, AND PAVING THE WAY FOR THOSE WHO COME AFTER US."

THE ROOTS

Daymond John began sharpening his entrepreneurial brain as early as first grade! He grew up in the Hollis, Queens, neighborhood of New York City during the rise of hip-hop. He was short, couldn't dance, and wasn't good at sports, but from a young age, he knew how to make money.

In elementary school, Daymond's first business was selling pencils. He took the paint off of ordinary pencils, and the girls at school would pay him to carve their names into the side. The pencils were a hit, and his customers were willing to pay double the price of a regular pencil! He raked leaves, shoveled snow, sold flyers for two dollars an hour, and even held his first job as an apprentice electrician at the age of ten. Daymond was a confident, inventive, natural entrepreneur, but he wouldn't understand the art of business until he was older.

Math and science were Daymond's best subjects in school, but he struggled with any subject that involved reading and writing. His dad thought he wasn't trying hard enough and would get mad and yell at him out of frustration. His school diagnosed him with a general "learning issue." He was eventually diagnosed with dyslexia as an adult, but it wasn't widely diagnosed nor understood when he was a kid.

Daymond's parents divorced, and his dad disappeared from their lives when he was ten years old. His mom worked three jobs to pay the bills. She used her busy schedule as an excuse to get Daymond to practice reading, asking him to read the highlights of the *New York Times* while she cooked and cleaned. This became their special Sunday ritual for several years.

In high school, Daymond had the opportunity to participate in his school's

"LISTEN, YOU'RE GOING TO HAVE TO FIGURE OUT WHAT YOU'RE DOING FOR THE REST OF YOUR LIFE, ONE WAY OR ANOTHER." —DAYMOND'S mom

co-op program, which allowed him to alternate weeks of full-time school with full-time work at an investment firm, where he learned a lot about business.

When his friends went to college and came back with degrees, Daymond realized he hadn't really made progress in his life. For most of Daymond's youth, he'd been waiting tables and hustling to make money, but he didn't necessarily enjoy the work he was doing.

But one day, Daymond's interest was sparked when he saw a nice-looking hat in Manhattan. He bought the hat and brought it home to his mom. He wanted to make some hats like it of his own to sell, so she offered to teach him how to sew. Eighty dollars' worth of fabric, some sewing, and time selling them on the streets turned into eight hundred dollars.

When he returned home after a successful day, he would do it all again, the next.

During this time, hip-hop was taking over the streets. Famous rappers were coming back home to Hollis, Queens, to see their family. It was inspiring to see the rise of local artists, and although Daymond couldn't rap or sing, he wanted to be a part of the scene. He thought that if hip-hop artists could tell their stories with words, he could do the same with clothing.

So, after hats came shirts, and before Daymond knew it, he had a business with three of his childhood friends—an apparel company called FUBU, which stands for "For Us, By Us." It was their way of celebrating the hip-hop community.

His mom's support was unwavering. To keep up with his rapidly growing business,

"I SEE THE WORLD IN A DIFFERENT WAY THAN MOST PEOPLE AND FOR ME, THAT'S BEEN A POSITIVE THING."

she gave him the money to fulfill orders and let him set up his factory in her basement. Music artists like LL Cool J, Will Smith, and Beyonce wore his shirts in their music videos, which gave his brand the exposure it needed to have an impact on hip-hop culture. When FUBU needed help financing, Daymond's mom helped him out again by finding a company to finance the fashion line. He signed a deal that stated he needed to sell $5 million worth of FUBU clothes in three years, which was worrisome, but he ended up selling $300 million worth of clothing in just three months!

His unique gift as a visual learner allowed him to map business plans in his head, and that, along with his entrepreneurial gift and determination, helped FUBU become one of the top clothing brands.

As texting and emailing replaced phone calls, Daymond's struggle with writing came back. Talking was easy for him, but spelling was the complete opposite, and people noticed. At the age of thirty, he was diagnosed with dyslexia, and all the trouble he'd always had finally made sense to him.

Since FUBU, Daymond has become a venture capitalist on the television show *Shark Tank*, and he's written three books. In 2015, President Barack Obama named him the Presidential Ambassador for Global Entrepreneurship.

Daymond is dedicated to spreading awareness and education about dyslexia, and as an entrepreneur and *Shark Tank* venture capitalist, he loves helping people make their big dreams come true.

JOY HARJO

AUTHOR + MUSICIAN

"I AM NOT SPECIAL. IT IS THE WAY FOR EVERYONE. WE ENTER INTO A FAMILY STORY, AND THEN OTHER STORIES BASED ON TRIBAL CLANS, ON TRIBAL TOWNS AND NATIONS, LANDS, COUNTRIES, PLANETARY SYSTEMS, AND UNIVERSES. YET WE EACH HAVE OUR OWN INDIVIDUAL SOUL STORY TO TEND."

t seems as though Joy Harjo was born with poetry in her mind, music in her bones, and art streaming from her body. She is a highly creative, gifted woman who was named US poet laureate in 2019.

Joy was born in 1951 in Tulsa, Oklahoma, and is a member of the Muscogee (Creek) Nation. At a young age, she felt very different from everyone around her. She was creative and sensitive. Her life felt like a jumble of puzzle pieces. It took many years for all her puzzle pieces to come together, but they eventually did in a magnificent way.

Joy began noticing her differences in school. She was told that she was a shy kid. She remembers enjoying painting because then she wouldn't have to speak. In school, she noticed that her drawings weren't like those of her classmates. She drew them from her imagination, but her classmates drew pictures that, to her, always looked the same. For example, in first grade, her class was drawing ghosts, and Joy drew a green ghost. Every child questioned her. Ghosts were supposed to be white, after all! She responded by asking them, "Have you ever seen a ghost?"

When Joy drew people, she'd make their skin orange, which was the closest color she could find among her crayons that matched her skin tone, but her Native American classmates didn't; she never understood why they left the skin color in their drawings colorless. Their skin and their culture were anything but plain.

Joy learned how to read in first grade. Reading was freedom to her. After she read every book in the first-grade class, she went on to read the second-grade collection. And for her eighth birthday, her mother bought Joy her first book of poetry, Louis Untermeyer's *Golden Books Family Treasury of Poetry*.

At home, Joy couldn't do the things she loved—art, sing, or dance. Her

IAIA
MUSEUM OF
CONTEMPORARY
NATIVE ARTS

home was often scary. Her dad was an alcoholic, and when he drank, it made him angry. Joy loved her dad, but she was also scared of him. Her mom got sick of the abuse, and her parents divorced. Her mom ended up remarrying a man who acted nice before the marriage. However, once they moved in with him, he was even more violent than her father.

The whole house feared her stepdad. There was no singing or dancing or after-school activities allowed. Just chores, silence, and fear. It was an awful way to live. But Joy found a way out. She heard about the Institute of American Indian Arts (IAIA) in Santa Fe, New Mexico, which, at the time, was a boarding school. She realized she could spend her high school years living at a school far

away from her horrendous home. She sent her application in with original sketches and cartoon drawings to IAIA and got accepted, allowing her to paint a new path.

Joy felt freedom at boarding school. She felt like New Mexico was home. Once a shy, fearful girl, she became someone who spoke up. She could paint, tell stories, act, and was able to shine. Her story was sad, scary, and lonely. But she found out that her story was common among her new friends. She discovered that a lot of her friends also came from scary homes, some even worse. Through creating art, some of them were able to heal.

The students not only were allowed to stay up late working on projects,

"WRITING POETRY IS A WAY TO TRANSFORM. IT'S BEEN A WAY TO TRANSFORM FEAR INTO SOMETHING USEFUL, TO TRANSFORM ANGER INTO SOMETHING THAT MIGHT HELP US MOVE FORWARD TOGETHER. THAT'S WHAT POETRY HAS BEEN FOR ME, AND FOR A LOT OF PEOPLE WORLDWIDE."

they were encouraged to! It felt good to finally be able to play music, perform in plays, and create art without fear. Joy's talent was immense, and she became an important part of her school community.

Joy graduated from IAIA, but then history began to repeat itself. She fell into the same rhythm as the women in her family and community. She stumbled into fearful and dangerous relationships. She spent a few years scraping by with her dreams crashing around her.

She eventually enrolled in the University of New Mexico, studying medicine and then switching to what she loved most—art. She received scholarships and earned excellent grades, but she still struggled with fear and anxiety. Then her first love, poetry,

gave her a voice. Once she was able to use poetry to face her fears and express her own struggles, the struggles of her ancestors, and those of her fellow Native Americans, there was no stopping her.

Joy went on to attend the University of Iowa and graduated with a master of fine arts. She has taught at IAIA, Arizona State University, the University of Colorado, the University of Arizona, and the University of New Mexico.

No longer jumbled, Joy's life became whole. Today she inspires many and thrives as a musician, artist, and poet. She and many other Native Americans have kept the history of their culture and memories of their ancestors alive through various forms of art, speaking for the past, to the present, and for the future.

Simone Biles is one of the best gymnasts the world has ever seen. She's so skilled in her craft that she invents new tricks at nearly every major competition. Her latest, the "Biles II," a triple-double, composed of a double backflip with three twists, has stunned spectators across the globe. She's tiny, fast, strong, and high energy!

Before her athleticism was discovered, Simone lived in an unstable environment with her younger sister, Adria. Luckily, her grandparents, who she refers to as her parents, saw the sisters' need for stability and adopted them. Simone and her sister grew up with them and their two sons, who they called their brothers, in Spring, Texas.

Born with energy just waiting to be unleashed, Simone ended up in the right place. Her older brother knew exactly what activities and games to play to help release at least some of her energy. One game they played was extending their arms out from their sides, acting as a pull-up bar, and they'd count how many pull-ups Simone could do on their arms! Simone would also jump from one couch to another and spring from bed to bed. She'd bounce on the family trampoline doing flip after flip for hours on end.

One day, Simone's brother stared outside at the pouring rain, trying to decide what to do. The day-care where he worked and where his sisters attended was supposed to go on a field trip to a farm. So he suggested they go to the nearby gymnastics center instead. Little did they know that introducing Simone to gymnastics would not only direct her energy, but would also ignite big dreams.

The minute Simone walked into the center, she copied the gymnasts who

"GIVEN HOW HYPER I WAS AS A KID, NO ONE WAS ENTIRELY SURPRISED WHEN IT TURNED OUT I HAD ADHD."

"THE FUNNY THING WAS, EVEN WITH ADHD, WHEN IT CAME TO GYMNASTICS, I WAS LASER FOCUSED."

were practicing. She went from one apparatus to the next. Her big brother challenged her to do a backflip, and after doing one, she did another but added a twist. One of the coaches observed Simone and was impressed with her defined muscles, energy, and natural ability, so she invited the sisters to join the gym.

Simone began gymnastics with raw talent. Her movements weren't refined because she had never had any training before, but she was able to do amazing things, like do a seat drop and bounce back on her feet like she was on a trampoline. After school, she'd head right to the gym to train.

Outside of gymnastics, Simone had a bubbly personality and a big smile. When she was excited to tell someone something, she couldn't hold her thoughts in. She had to tell them

everything right then and there at warp speed. School was a fun place to socialize, but it was full of distractions making it hard for her to focus.

When Simone was in seventh grade, her parents took her to get tested for learning differences. Ultimately, she was diagnosed with ADHD. In Simone's case, it resulted in hyperactivity and difficulty with focusing on tasks, especially ones she was uninterested in. Although it made being a student difficult, ADHD gave Simone what she calls her superpowers: unmatched energy and the ability to focus on something she had an intense interest in for long periods of time—gymnastics!

To compete with the best gymnasts in the world, Simone made the difficult decision to homeschool. Her training hours jumped from twenty hours a week to more than thirty-five hours a week!

Before long, the extra hours paid off, and Simone was winning the World Championships and other big competitions. She began to think that maybe, just maybe, she had a chance to go to the 2016 Summer Olympic Games in Rio de Janeiro, Brazil. Between her training, her energy, and her laser focus, Simone made the team! She and the other members of the US women's artistic gymnastics team won the gold, and silver and bronze medals, making them the most decorated American gymnastics team ever!

As Simone prepared for her next Olympic Games, she had to confront and deal with some horrific events. Simone and at least 156 other female students and young athletes came forward and testified that one of the most famous doctors in gymnastics sexually abused them. In total, 265 women and girls ultimately spoke out about their experiences. The doctor pled guilty and is in jail for the rest of his life.

While the experiences she suffered weighed on her, Simone was able to compete in the 2020 Summer Olympic Games in Tokyo, Japan, which, due to the COVID-19 pandemic, took place in 2021. There, Simone earned two more medals but had to pull out of most of her events due to "the twisties," a scary condition common in gymnasts where they can't tell up from down. She spoke out about her mental health and pressure to perform well for everyone. Simone was embraced by the world with love and support for her bravery and again for speaking her truth.

Simone may have a combined total of thirty-two World Championships and Olympic medals, but her spirit and ability to speak out about the mental wellness and safety of athletes is a profound and lasting legacy.

"I'M NOT THE NEXT USAIN BOLT OR MICHAEL PHELPS, I'M THE FIRST SIMONE BILES."

ongresswoman Ayanna Pressley represents Massachusetts's Seventh Congressional District in the US House of Representatives. Her work focuses on the health and wellness of children, families, and communities because the support of her own community is what helped her become the woman she is today.

Ayanna grew up in Chicago, Illinois, and was raised by her mother, Sandra, who was a social worker, community organizer, and legal secretary. Her activism had a huge influence on her daughter, as the world would later learn. Although Sandra was a strong and independent woman, she was in an abusive relationship during Ayanna's childhood. Ayanna was not only living in a stressful environment, but she had also been sexually abused.

The harm she experienced was traumatizing. It overwhelmed her, causing her to shut down. In addition to the harm she experienced, Ayanna's dad was absent for most of her childhood. He had a drug addiction and was in and out of jail for many years.

Despite their challenging home life, Ayanna's mom was determined to give Ayanna the best opportunities she could. She worked three jobs, but they often didn't have enough money for daily living. As an adult looking back at this time in her life, Ayanna has said, "It was

"IT WAS ME AND HER VERSUS THE REST OF THE WORLD. CAGNEY AND LACEY. THELMA AND LOUISE."

me and her versus the rest of the world. Cagney and Lacey. Thelma and Louise."

Ayanna received a partial scholarship to Francis W. Parker School from kindergarten through high school. This school was a safe community for Ayanna. She dealt with her challenges by being quiet and hardly speaking to anyone. The school community supported her, especially the school nurse, who identified the signs of abuse in Ayanna. The school became the safe place for her to heal and help her become the formidable woman she is today.

She thrived in this supportive environment. Ayanna became a cheerleader, competitive debater, student government president, commencement speaker, and class salutatorian. When she graduated from high school, Ayanna

was named most likely to become mayor of Chicago!

With all the struggles Ayanna and her mother faced, Sandra was able to build confidence, love, and strength in Ayanna. In return, Ayanna grew into a strong, smart leader. She was different in many ways—the only Black person in her school, a survivor of abuse, and a young woman who truly wanted to change the world.

After high school, Ayanna attended Boston University and joined as many activities as possible. She was elected student president and student senator in her first year. She had fun, made friends, and was on a good path.

Life is like a roller coaster, though. Lots of ups, downs, twists, and turns. In college, Ayanna was forced into a particular challenge that changed the

"SHE HAD HER OWN FAMILY STRUGGLES, BUT SHE FOUND AT PARKER A PLACE THAT WOULD NOT ONLY SUPPORT HER BUT GIVE HER AN OPPORTUNITY TO BE SOMETHING OTHER THAN A KID WHO HAD STRUGGLES AT HOME. HERE, SHE COULD JUST BE, AND GROW, AND DEVELOP, AND HAVE A VOICE"
—DANIEL B. FRANK
FRANCIS W. PARKER SCHOOL PRINCIPAL

course of her life. Her mom lost her job, and Ayanna made the decision to drop out of college to support and provide for her mom.

After working a few different jobs, she had the opportunity to work as a senior aide to Representative Joseph P. Kennedy II and as a political director for Senator John Kerry. She enjoyed the work, but left her job with Senator Kerry so she could run for Boston City Council. She won and became the first Black woman to serve on the council!

In 2018, she forged on in her political career when she was elected to serve Massachusetts's Seventh Congressional District in the US House of Representatives, becoming the first Black woman to be elected to Congress from the Commonwealth of Massachusetts.

Ayanna continues to proudly serve her district in Congress, working to bring value and balance to her community. She strives to put the health and wellness of families and communities first in her work. As a leader, Ayanna joins progressive Congress representatives Ilhan Omar, Alexandria Ocasio-Cortez a.k.a. AOC, Rashida Tlaib, Jamaal Bowman, and Cori Bush, known as "The Squad," as well as others in positions of power in local and national governments, in the quest for equality and equity in our country.

I BELIEVE YOU NEED STRONG AND HEALTHY FAMILIES TO HAVE STRONG AND HEALTHY COMMUNITIES TO HAVE A STRONG AND HEALTHY CITY.

AYANNA PRESSLEY CONGRESS

AYANNA PRESSLEY FOR CONGRESS

AYANNA

THE ECOSYSTEM I'M WORKING INTENTIONALLY TO CREATE AND TO FOSTER BEGINS WITH FAMILY. AND I VIEW EVERY ISSUE THROUGH THE LENS OF HEALTH AND EQUITY."

Temple Grandin was born in 1947 in Boston, Massachusetts. When she was just a baby, her mom knew something wasn't quite right. Most babies start babbling around nine months old and say their first word by age one. But Temple didn't utter a word till she was three and a half years old.

Baby Temple also didn't like to be touched. She didn't look at people even if they were talking to her, and loud noises and bright lights caused her pain. All this stimulation resulted in tantrums. Her mother sensed that Temple's brain worked differently. Doctors eventually diagnosed her with autism and suggested she be sent to live in an institution.

Absolutely horrified at the thought of sending her daughter off to a place away from family, her mom was determined to give Temple a life worth living. It wasn't an easy path, as autism caused Temple to have little control over her frustration, anxiety, and anger. When her emotions were too big for her to handle, she'd melt down by yelling or throwing things.

She was teased and bullied by classmates because she thought differently, acted differently, and understood things differently. But sometimes she'd retaliate against her bullies. When she was fourteen, she threw a book at a classmate for teasing her and was consequently expelled. She was misunderstood among her peers and teachers. Horseback riding, building model rockets, and working with electronics were some of her favorite things to do. When she was doing these things with people who also liked these things, she felt like she fit in.

Although acceptable behavior was her challenge, school was a place where she eventually excelled. She was often very bored in school and goofed around a lot. No one understood how her brain worked or how to teach her. Eventually, one teacher figured her out. Her high school math teacher, Mr. Carlock, had worked for NASA before becoming a teacher, and after spending time getting to know Temple, he could tell that she was gifted. He was able to challenge her with special building projects that suited her talents. Her unique ability allowed her to plan and build things entirely in her head before she built them in the real world. Mr. Carlock took the time to understand her, built her confidence, and became the mentor Temple needed.

As a teenager, Temple spent many summers at her aunt's cattle ranch in Arizona. Temple's relationship with her aunt and the ranch had a huge impact on her. She enjoyed watching the cows. Temple noticed the things that upset the cows and the things that calmed them. She discovered that she could picture in her mind what it was like to be a cow. She could imagine how a cow could feel, better than she could for any human.

One thing Temple noticed when she was paying close attention was the "squeeze chute," which was a special cage with sides that gently pressed against the sides of cows to calm them down before getting shots. One day, Temple got really upset and couldn't calm herself down, so she crawled inside the squeeze chute and pulled the lever. When the cage walls gently squeezed her sides, she felt calm and relaxed, just like the cows.

"THE WORLD NEEDS ALL KINDS OF MINDS..."

At college, she struggled with anxiety and how different she was from everyone else. She didn't like having a roommate, and classmates teased her for her unusual behavior. To ease her discomfort, she built her very own "squeeze machine." However, the college thought it was odd, and they made her take it apart.

That didn't stop Temple, though. She proposed testing her squeeze machine on her classmates as an official experiment to see how they reacted to it. The college agreed, and Temple launched her first scientific study. Through her experiment, she discovered that her invention calmed many people—even people without autism!

Temple furthered her education at graduate school to study animal science. She was interested in researching cows and their behavior. She thought there were ways to make them feel safe and comfortable and still allow the ranchers to do their jobs. She used her unique gift to imagine how it felt to be a cow on a ranch and what things humans could do to make life calmer and happier for the cows.

Despite the disapproval ranchers had toward women working on the ranch, especially one as different as Temple, she proved to them that her ideas would not only decrease their cows stress but also improve the rancher's workflow. She designed equipment that helped keep the cows moving happily and calmly. When ranchers saw the positive effect Temple's equipment had on the cows, they stopped treating Temple so poorly.

Temple earned a PhD in animal science, became a professor of animal science at Colorado State University, an autism activist, and a bestselling author. In 2010, *Time* magazine voted her one of the 100 Most Influential People in the world.

The only man to be an air traffic controller, Navy SEAL, and Army Ranger, David Goggins has become one of the toughest men alive. David wasn't born with innate physical and mental toughness. He had to overcome challenges in his own way to gain this strength.

David, his brother, and his mother were abused by his father during his early life. As with many kids who suffer from abuse, David struggled in all the areas he was supposed to be growing in.

When David was eight years old, he and his mom escaped his dad's wrath, while his older brother decided to stay with their dad. They settled in a small town in Indiana, where they were one of the few Black families in town. David may have been safe from his dad, but he now experienced harmful and sometimes terrifying acts of racism. It never got easy, and it never went away; he had to coexist with it.

These stressful years caused David to develop a stutter, and on top of that, he didn't know how to read. His confidence dropped with each mounting challenge. The only way he felt he could handle his learning challenge was to cheat in school, but that didn't help him in the long run.

He trudged through his days, unsure of his purpose in life. He made poor decisions and put in little effort at school. He let everything discourage him from achieving any sort of success. His mom didn't know how to get through to him, and by the time he was in high school, she was too tired to even care.

Inspired by his grandfather's service in the air force, David joined the Civil Air Patrol. Through this program, he learned about Pararescue and wanted to be one of those people jumping out of airplanes. It did take David several failing report cards and being cut from the basketball team for him to realize he was wasting his opportunity to be a Pararescueman.

When he found out he was failing school and no one seemed to care, he decided to care. He walked to the bathroom and stared at himself in the mirror. He named it the Accountability Mirror. Looking at his reflection, he realized that he was the only person who could change his course. He was the only person who could make life better for himself.

Once he began taking charge of his life, his mom hired a tutor to help teach him how to read and study. His hard work began to pay off when he made the basketball team in his senior year, made good enough grades to graduate high school, and even passed the air force written exam!

After the air force, he worked as a pest exterminator. It wasn't his dream job. In fact, his work made him constantly sad. He had gained a lot of weight and wasn't inspired to do anything. But on one fateful day, he watched a program that followed a group of Navy SEALs (Sea, Air, and Land), and a new dream was born.

His first attempt at completing the SEALs' grueling twenty-four-week training course ended early with double pneumonia, and the second attempt ended early with a severely injured knee. He knew he had only one more shot

at becoming a SEAL, so he took time off to heal his body and his mind not only from the injuries but also from his childhood trauma.

His third round of training was just as brutal as ever, but David stayed focused and positive. When even his bones started breaking, he wrapped up his legs, laced up his boots, and pushed himself to the end. David graduated with class 235 and was granted the opportunity to begin his Navy SEAL duties. He was so happy and so proud of himself.

On top of becoming a Navy SEAL chief, David also became a US Army Ranger, another military special operations force. But over the years of service, David had a lot of friends who died or came back wounded from missions. Families were devastated by the loss of their loved ones in service. David wanted to ease some of their suffering and do something for the families of his fellow fallen warriors. Running races seemed like the best way for him to raise money for these families, so without any specific running training, he signed up for the San Diego One Day, 24-hour ultramarathon. His goal was to compete and raise money for the Special Operations Warrior Foundation. Running this race was harder for him than Navy SEAL training. With broken bones, fatigue, and in dire need of a hospital, David finished the event!

David has now competed in over sixty ultramarathons and has the Guinness World Record for the most pull-ups in twenty-four hours—4,030! Living his motto, "Stay Hard," David's success has come from pushing through his discomfort and strengthening his body and mind. He was never trying to be better than anyone around him, just be better than himself every day.

"I CAME FROM NOTHING. BUT THE THING ABOUT IT IS...

WE ALL HAVE THE ABILITY TO COME FROM NOTHING TO SOMETHING. BUT IT TAKES THAT KIND OF SPIRIT."

J osh Fernandez is both quiet and loud. He observes, and he takes action. His indomitable spirit has both created problems and created opportunity. No one knew that this angry, brokenhearted kid would turn into a man who gives to others and encourages people from all walks of life to be themselves and to chase their dreams—not even Josh.

His early childhood days were spent romping around the streets of Boston, Massachusetts, with his friend, Joe Grand. Their lifelong bond grew from feeling like outsiders, supporting each other's gifts, and from some mischief-making!

Life was going well for Josh until his family moved to a new neighborhood. He suddenly had new neighbors, a new school, and new classmates. His familiar world was replaced during an important stage of child development.

On one of his first days at his new school, his teacher gave the class an exercise called Mad Minute Math. The goal was to do as many math problems as possible in one minute. Josh froze. He was so worried and scared that he couldn't do the work. He couldn't write one answer down. He was filled with anxiety as he stared at the math sheet. This single math assignment marked the beginning of Josh's educational trauma and his plummeting confidence. He felt sad and dumb.

Josh was placed in special education math. On his first day of class, running late, he tripped and his pencil pierced through his hand—an accident he perceived as a failure. Everything he was doing in school seemed to be wrong and just added to his negative thoughts about himself.

"my mom was telling me I WASN'T NORMAL. A LOT OF PEOPLE WERE TELLING ME I WASN'T NORMAL.

BUT WHO CARES ABOUT NORMAL? I THINK IT'S MORE IMPORTANT TO BE YOURSELF."

Josh loved writing silly poems and stories, but most of all, he loved surrounding himself with books. So he started skipping school and sneaking off to the ultimate sanctuary—the public library. His comforting escape ended after a few weeks. He got caught and was forced to return to school. His teachers and parents were angry and annoyed with him. Every adult kept telling him that he was messing everything up and ruining his future.

His family moved to Sacramento, California, when he was in middle school, and his negative attitude and growing anger moved with him. He felt either sad or mad, with the only happiness coming from the time he spent with his baby sister.

When Josh was fifteen, his little sister began having stomach complications. His family couldn't get the help she needed quickly enough, and she died. What joy he had disappeared with her death. The school and family trauma he suffered made him angrier. His parents were also upset with him because they didn't understand him or know how to help him.

For many years, the effects of Josh's childhood trauma stuck with him. He comforted himself by using drugs. He became addicted to them and made a lot of bad choices. He dropped out of high school and never graduated.

Although Josh always felt different and lived in constant emotional pain, he did have another outlet besides drugs. He had writing. To Josh, writing felt like a spiritual experience. It guided him.

Josh spent a lot of time writing poems and submitting them to contests and publications, but his submissions were rejected. One day, an old girlfriend got sick of him wasting his life and signed him up for community college. Josh decided to go, and there he met a professor who would change his life.

Jan was Josh's English professor at Sacramento City College. After he turned in a writing assignment that she loved, she told him he had talent and needed to keep writing. Jan wouldn't let him fail. She gave him responsibilities, opportunities, and the one thing he needed—someone to believe in him!

Soon after, he wanted to make lasting change. He remembered the times he went running with his friend Joe and how good it made him feel and the hope it gave him. So Josh laced up his running shoes and gave it a shot. Running made his body feel good, and he realized that if he wanted to get up in the morning to run, he couldn't drink alcohol or do drugs. Running's positive effects outperformed any other old habit and desire.

Through Josh's practice of healthful habits and behaviors, he was able to take charge of his life. Once he healed, his dreams began to come true—he became a published poet, professional writer, English professor, and earned a master's degree!

Josh uses his skills, his position, and his voice to make a difference where he can. He collects and brings food and clothing to the houseless on a regular basis and fights for justice by being a positive voice against racism. Josh also teaches English in prisons and helps inmates reenter society. Josh experienced firsthand how people can overcome challenges, and he wants to inspire others as well.

The first comic strip printed in newspaper form was written in 1895. The simple, humorous style used in these comic strips not only sold a lot of papers but also helped immigrants moving to the United States learn how to read! Funny pictures were also Dav Pilkey's gateway into language. He'd look at pictures and try to decode the words alongside them to understand the story. The more he read, the better he got. Known for his comics and graphic novels, Dav is one of the funniest and most talented children's book authors.

Dav, who grew up in Cleveland, Ohio, is dyslexic, which makes reading and writing a struggle. When Dav was growing up, dyslexia wasn't widely understood. Teachers didn't know how to teach a child with dyslexia.

Teachers told Dav that he was dumb, and he felt dumb too. Unlike the other kids in his class, his reading level was behind his classmates. They dreaded listening to him read aloud because it took him so long. Teachers openly compared his reading and writing to a baby's. His teachers' words stung worse than a bee.

Dyslexia was just one of Dav's struggles in school. The other struggle was attention deficit hyperactivity disorder (ADHD), which Dav calls "attention deficit hyperactivity delightfulness." ADHD is a developmental disorder that affects both kids and adults.

"ATTENTION DEFICIT HYPERACTIVITY DELIGHTFULNESS."

Dav couldn't read, and he couldn't sit still in his seat, pay attention, or control his impulses, like making farting noises with his armpit! What he could do, though, was draw and write funny comics—misspellings 'n' all. Making comics was his way of communicating with the world. His paper and pencils didn't judge him; they allowed him to be himself. Instead of being known as the kid who got sent out of the class or the kid who couldn't read, he was the funny kid who could draw!

Every day in school, Dav knew that he would be unable to control the impulse to disrupt class and would be sent out to the hallway. At first, Dav would roam the hallways. He'd sneak into classrooms and write funny messages on the chalkboards when no one was looking. His teacher eventually realized what he was doing and put a desk outside the classroom just for him.

Luckily, he was able to sneak some paper and pencils into the lift-up desk.

It was at this desk where Dav's comics took off. His classmates may not have been thrilled when it was his turn to read aloud, but they loved when he shared his comics. These moments were like a test to discover which drawings and words would bring the most laughter.

One day during class, his teacher made the mistake of saying the word "underwear"! The entire class roared with laughter and gave Dav the idea for his new comic book character, Captain Underpants! However, Dav's comics weren't understood by his school principal or teachers.

They were more than just negative toward his comics; they were outright mean. They ripped up his drawings, called him names, and punished him with a paddle. The adults at his school thought that physical punishment would bring good behavior. They were wrong. Instead of squashing Dav's creativity, their treatment inspired the characters and stories he writes about today.

Dav had amazing parents. They didn't get mad at him for misbehaving, and they didn't make him feel bad for not being able to read well. They gave him endless love and support. His mom encouraged him to read whatever was interesting to him, from comic strips to the *Guinness World Records*. When he'd come home discouraged from school, his mom would say, "Everything happens for a reason. Maybe something good will come out of this." His parents allowed him to be himself, and they encouraged Dav's creativity by requesting their very own series that Dav named Water Man—a man who could do anything that water could do!

In high school, Dav continued to feel like an outsider. His principal told him that he'd never make a living as an artist. While school continued to be a negative place for him, his parents' unyielding support kept him going He entered his freshman year of college at Kent State University as an art major, and there, he had his first positive encounter in an educational setting. An English professor noticed his impressive writing and drawing abilities and suggested that he become a children's book author. In 1986, he won a national competition with his book *World War Won*! It was a turning point in his life, but it wasn't suddenly smooth sailing. Dav got rejected over twenty-three times for one of his first books—but that didn't stop him. He persevered and, in time, worked to have a successful career writing funny books for kids.

P!nk flies, flips, and sings through sold-out arenas worldwide. She moves through the air while suspended from ceilings using a flying harness, silks, and bungee cords. She is a powerhouse singer-songwriter who has sold more than sixty million albums! Before she became P!nk, the mega pop star, she was young Alecia Moore, who had to find her way through a challenging childhood.

Alecia's early childhood was spent running barefoot through the forest in her backyard and riding bikes with her brother. The two siblings were on their own much of the time because their parents worked and their mom went to school when she wasn't working. Still, their parents had time to give them unconditional love.

But when her parents grew unhappy in their marriage, their unhappiness would turn into yelling. It made Alecia sad and angry. When the fighting got bad, she'd fold herself into a small ball and cover her ears.

She liked to sing and write and found that these two things made her feel good, so they became her escape. She wrote a poem about how she felt about her parents' divorce, and later that poem became a song on her album *M!ssundaztood*.

At the age of nine, Alecia began taking singing lessons, and at the year-end recital, she performed in front of a live audience. Alecia commanded the stage in front of 1,500 people. As she sung the last verse of her song, she turned her back to the crowd, faced the band, stretched her arms out wide, and with a bow of her head, the song ended. The crowd clapped and cheered, and her parents

"SINGING WAS THE ONLY WAY THAT I COULD GET PEOPLE TO STOP TALKING AND LISTEN TO ME.

IT WAS THE ONLY WAY THAT I COULD GET MY PARENTS TO STOP FIGHTING."

"MY TEACHERS HATED ME BECAUSE I WAS CURIOUS... [BUT] I WAS ALSO CONFRONTATIONAL. I HAD A CHIP ON MY SHOULDER. I WAS REALLY SMART AND I WAS REALLY HURTING."

knew that Alecia Moore of Doylestown, Pennsylvania, was meant to sing.

Writing and singing helped Alecia, but she moved through the world with anger and sadness because of her parents' failed marriage. She also witnessed her brother get severely bullied, and she fought back for him. Her strong will was a great attribute, but most people didn't think so at the time.

She got kicked out of Catholic Sunday school because she questioned whether Jesus was Jewish. She got kicked out of Brownies, and she also got kicked out of gymnastics, which was one of her favorite things to do. Once more, her feisty personality got in the way.

Alecia began smoking cigarettes before she was in middle school, and when she was eleven, she started smoking marijuana. By the time she was twelve, she was using drugs.

Taking drugs altered Alecia's mind. She painted her room black, snuck out of the house nearly every night, and fought

with her mom constantly. Eventually, her mom was exhausted by Alecia's behavior and kicked her out of the house, forcing Alecia to move in with her dad.

Even though she had a great relationship with her dad, Alecia would still sneak out of the house and escape to nightclubs. One night, while out at a club Alecia's friends passed her a microphone and she sang. The popular Philadelphia DJ, DJ Storm, loved what he heard and said he'd give her the guest spotlight but only if she was drug-free.

Alecia seized the opportunity. She returned the next night to a crowd who didn't want to hear from a teenage white girl, but she fought back with her gifted voice and won over the crowd! Alecia never did drugs again.

One night she was discovered while performing at the nightclub. At first, she was a part of a group, but then she was encouraged to go solo. Alecia didn't want to leave her group, but she decided to give it a try—this is when Alecia became P!nk. She signed a contract and took the spotlight.

People in charge didn't want her to be herself, but she knew they were wrong. She dressed the way she wanted, wrote the lyrics she wanted, and sang the way she wanted. She wouldn't change for anyone, and it paid off because music fans loved her just the way she was.

Her M!ssundaztood album catapulted her career. On this album, she had the opportunity to work with her childhood idol, Linda Perry, who helped her write about her life experiences and how they made her feel. P!nk went into the recording booth, and twenty minutes later, her song "Family Portrait" was written.

In November 2017, at the MTV Video Music Awards (VMAs), P!nk received Billboard's Icon Award and the Video Vanguard Award, an award for making a profound impact on music video culture. In her acceptance speech, she emphasized that it's OK to be different and no one should change for anyone.

P!nk is married and has two children, who she raises to be strong, courageous, and kind with themselves and others. She's won several awards for her music, has a star on the Hollywood Walk of Fame, and fifteen of her singles have been in the top ten of Billboard Hot 100 chart. P!nk believes that we all go through struggles and, by sharing our stories, we can heal and grow.

"I SIGNED UP FOR THIS LIFE BEFORE I GOT HERE. I CHOSE IT. I CHOSE ALL THE OBSTACLES AS WELL. I CHOSE ALL THE CHALLENGES. I CHOSE ALL THE PAIN OF MY CHILDHOOD, WHICH WOULD EVENTUALLY BRING ME TO BE ABLE TO WRITE THE KINDS OF SONGS AND FEEL THE KINDS OF EMOTIONS AND NOT BE AFRAID OF PAIN TO DO WHAT I DO."

AFTERWORD
NOTE TO GROWN-UPS

You may know a young person who is struggling in a similar way to someone in this book, and hopefully, the stories told have helped to bring additional understanding. Sometimes a kid stands on their desk in the middle of a lesson because they don't know what to do with the anxiety that floods inside of them. Sometimes a kid withdraws so silently, you forget they are there. Maybe they have a learning challenge or an adverse childhood experience. Maybe a kid just feels different and struggles to communicate with their peers. Whatever is going on, it doesn't have to hold them back. With the proper support, they can thrive. Kids need to know that they aren't alone, there are people who can help them, and it's going to be OK. I think that's the biggest worry for grown-ups—will this young person be OK? Will they see that despite the troublemaker(s) in their life, they possess a uniqueness that's even more powerful? Will they keep on striving toward their dreams despite having to overcome certain challenges?

More often than not, we will all come up against something that tests us. The hope is that there is a support system for us to lean on and use to help us get through the hard times. Therapists, teachers, family members, doctors, and so many others are equipped to be of service all in their own ways. It's our job to use the resources, speak up, and get young people the help they need to feel successful and proud of who they are growing to be.

In strength and support,
MARISELA VAN SICKLE, LCSW

RESOURCES

ADDICTION
www.adolescenthealth.org/resources/clinical-care-
  resources.aspx

ADHD
www.additudemag.com
chadd.org

ADVERSE CHILDHOOD EXPERIENCES
centerforyouthwellness.org/the-science/
childtrauma.org

ANXIETY
childmind.org/topics/concerns/anxiety/

AUTISM
www.autismspeaks.org/what-autism
www.autism-society.org

DYSLEXIA
dyslexia.yale.edu
childmind.org/guide/quick-guide-to-dyslexia/

FOSTER CARE
jillana-goble.com

LEARNING DIFFERENCES
www.ldrfa.org

MENTAL HEALTH HOTLINE
988lifeline.org/
www.mentalhealth.gov/get-help/immediate-help

OCD
iocdf.org/about-ocd/
www.psychiatry.org/patients-families/
  obsessive-compulsive-disorder

INDEX

A

abuse, 80, 83–84, 101, 103, 104, 111
Aderin-Pocock, Maggie, 10–13
ADHD (attention deficit hyperactivity disorder), 15–17, 33, 39–41, 47–48, 63, 100, 119–120
anxiety, 22–25, 33, 84, 97, 109
AOC (Alexandria Ocasio-Cortez), 105
Asperger's syndrome, 56, 73
autism, 56, 73, 106–109
Awkwafina (Nora Lum), 46–49

B

Beyonce, 93
Big Daddy Kane, 88
Biles, Simone, 98–101
Black Thought (Tariq Trotter), 86–89
Bowman, Jamaal, 105
Breton, André, 37
Brewer, Hamish, 66–69
Bukowski, Charles, 48
bullying, 19, 43, 45, 55–56, 76, 107
Bush, Cori, 105

C

Carlock, Mr., 108
Cho, Margaret, 48
Coach Bob, 40–41
Cooper, Bobb, 24
Cooper, Ilene, 45
Corn, Seane, 82–85

D

depression, 41, 63, 81
DJ Storm, 124
Dunne, Gary, 20
dyslexia, 11, 13, 91, 93, 119–120

E

Eminem, 19

F

Fernandez, Josh, 75, 114–117
Foxx, Jamie, 21
FUBU, 92–93

G

Goggins, David, 110–113
Golden, Jane, 88
Grammafina, 47

Grand, Joe, 74–77, 115
Grandin, Temple, 106–109
Green, John, 42–45

H

Hamilton, Charles, 29
Harjo, Joy, 94–97
Herrera, Bobby, 58–61
Hughes, Langston, 29

J

John, Daymond, 90–93
John, Elton, 21
Johnson, Lyndon B., 29
JVN (Jonathan Van Ness), 78–81

K

Kahlo, Frida, 34–37, 68
Kennedy, Jackie, 53
Kennedy, John F., 50–53
Kennedy, Joseph P., II, 105
Kerry, John, 105
keywords, 7–8
King, Martin Luther, Jr., 29, 68
Kingpin, 75
Kool G Rap, 88

L

LL Cool J, 93
Lum, Nora (a.k.a. Awkwafina), 46–49

M

Mandel, Howie, 30–33
Marshall, Thurgood, 26–29
Marzo, Clay, 70–73
mental health, 41, 81, 88, 101
Moore, Alecia (a.k.a. P!nk), 122–125

N

Noah, Trevor, 62–65

O

Obama, Barack, 68, 93
obsessive-compulsive disorder (OCD), 32, 33, 42–45, 56, 84, 85
Ocasio-Cortez, Alexandria (a.k.a. AOC), 105
Omar, Ilhan, 105

P

Parks, Rosa, 29
Perry, Linda, 125

Phelps, Michael, 38–41
Pilkey, Dav, 118–121
P!nk (Alecia Moore), 122–125
post-traumatic stress disorder (PTSD), 88
Pressley, Ayanna, 102–105

Q

Questlove (Ahmir Thompson), 89

R

racism, 26–29, 53, 64–65, 111
Rakim, 88
Rice, Damien, 20
Rivera, Diego, 37
Rogen, Seth, 49

S

Schoolly D, 88
sexual abuse, 80, 83–84, 101, 103, 104
Sheeran, Ed, 18–21
Smith, Will, 93
St. John, George, 52
Stewart, Jon, 65
Stone, Emma, 22–25
stutter, 19, 111
substance abuse, 41, 81, 116, 117, 124

T

Thompson, Ahmir (a.k.a. Questlove), 89
Thunberg, Greta, 54–57
Tlaib, Rashida, 105
Trotter, Tariq (a.k.a. Black Thought), 86–89

U

Untermeyer, Louis, 95

V

Van Ness, Jonathan (a.k.a. JVN), 78–81
Victorino, Shane, 14–17

W

Wald, Doug, 25

ABOUT THE AUTHOR AND ILLUSTRATOR

KEELY GRAND is a mom, author, personal trainer, and wellness specialist. Her interest in people, specifically their health, gifts, and challenges, was sparked by years of trying to find ways to connect with her younger cousin who lived with severe cerebral palsy. She earned a master's degree in health communication from Emerson College and has worked as a community health educator, a cross country and track coach, and freelance writer. Diagnosed in adulthood with anxiety and ADHD, she manages her own troublemakers through exercise, speaking with a therapist, and practicing yoga.

RAGON DICKARD is a Seattle-based illustrator who loves to make art with monsters, animals, people, fruits, and vegetables. Ragon is inspired by folk art, printmaking, animation, and kitschy things at thrift stores. You can find out more about her on her website, RagonDickard.com.